A *Singular Manual* of
TEXTBOOK PREPARATION

Second Edition

■ M. N. HEGDE, Ph.D. ■

California State University-Fresno

SINGULAR PUBLISHING GROUP, INC.
SAN DIEGO • LONDON

Singular Publishing Group, Inc.
401 West A Street, Suite 325
San Diego, California 92101-7904

20 Compton Terrace
London, N1 2UN, U.K.

Second Edition
© 1996 by Singular Publishing Group, Inc.
Typeset in Garamond by CFW Graphics.
Printed in the United States of America by McNaughton & Gunn, Inc.

Library of Congress Cataloging-in-Publication Data

Hegde, M. N. (Mahabalagiri N.), 1941-
    A Singular manual of textbook preparation / M.N. Hegde.—2nd ed.
      p.   cm.
    Includes bibliographical references (p.   ) and index.
    ISBN 1-56593-640-X
    1. Textbooks—Authorship—Handbooks, manuals, etc. 2. Textbooks—Publishing—Handbooks, manuals, etc.   I. Title.
LB3045.5.H44 1996
371.3'2—dc20   96-10283
                                                        CIP

Table of Contents

■ CHAPTER 3

WRITING STYLE 21

■ CHAPTER 4

PREPARATION AND DELIVERY OF A TEXTBOOK 29

Foreword

I said in the *Forword* to the first edition that this would be a very useful book for those who plan to write professional books. The advent of the second edition is proof enough that the first edition did its job. It served as a guide to hundreds of authors in an area where not much help is available, leading them from conceptualization to outline, to adherence, to details in completing a manuscript to meet a publisher's expectations.

This revised and expanded second edition, including the most current APA style guidelines, is right on target as a guide to textbook preparation for students of the next century. It is written for advanced graduate students preparing to write formal papers, theses, and dissertations; but most importantly, it is an invaluable book for *anyone* who wants to write a successful textbook.

Sadanand Singh, Ph.D.
Chairman
Singular Publishing Group, Inc.

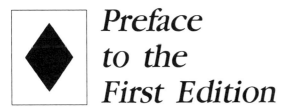

Preface to the First Edition

This *Manual* is written for authors who write textbooks for courses taught at colleges and universities. It may seem unnecessary for the accomplished writer. Still, many authors have questions about the organization, content, style, and other aspects of textbook writing. Therefore, this *Manual* is offered as a ready source of information on various aspects of textbook writing and publishing.

This *Manual* should not discourage innovative writing styles. We hope to incorporate authors' many creative ideas for organizing and writing texts into the *Manual* as it is periodically revised.

The purpose of providing this *Manual* to authors is to describe some essential features of successful textbooks and to ensure a somewhat uniform organization of manuscripts. The *Manual* addresses such matters as content, style, format, editorial reviews, and production of texts. Texts prepared according to the suggestions offered in this *Manual* will save everyone time, effort, and expenses. Our purpose will be served if a few authors find this *Manual* helpful in writing and publishing their textbooks.

Preface to the Second Edition

Feedback received from many textbook authors on the first edition of this *Manual* has indicated that it has been helpful in preparing textbook manuscripts. I am thankful to all those who have given me positive feedback and constructive suggestions for improvement.

In this second edition, information on electronic manuscript preparation has been updated. A new chapter on general writing style has been added (Chapter 3). Chapter 7, new for this edition, describes preparation of revised editions of texts. Chapter 6 has been rewritten to give detailed information on production of textbooks. I hope that authors of textbooks for higher education will continue to find this *Manual* useful and easy to use.

This revision has been greatly enhanced by the feedback provided by Singular Publishing Group's copy editors Sandy Doyle and Randy Stevens. Angie Singh, President of Singular Publishing Group, who also heads its production department, has provided much useful information on the book production process. Textbook writers may find this expanded second edition more useful than its predecessor because of their expert help. I am grateful to them.

1 | *Writing a Textbook Proposal*

■ IF YOU WISH TO SEND A TEXTBOOK PROPOSAL

Contact an Editor

When you have an idea for a text, but have not written any chapters of the book, you should contact the publishing house of your choice and discuss your ideas with an editor. The editor who is interested in your proposal will invite you to send a book proposal.

Some publishing houses have consulting editors or textbook series editors who help acquire and edit books for them. Consulting and series editors are typically not housed in publishing companies. They are your colleagues in universities. You also may contact such an editor who might invite you to send a book proposal. If the consulting or the series editor finds your proposal worthwhile, he or she will make a positive recommendation to the publisher. If the publisher accepts your proposal, you would then start working with the consulting or series editor and the in-house editor.

Sometimes, publishers invite potential authors to consider writing a textbook. Those who accept this invitation also should write a comprehensive book proposal for the editors to evaluate.

Make a Market Analysis

Plan your book proposal carefully and thoughtfully. Before you write the proposal, do the following:

■ Evaluate your competition. Study the books on the market to assess their strengths and weaknesses.

■ Design a book that overcomes the weaknesses of competing books while not sacrificing their strengths.

■ Design a unique book that will contain creative teaching devices not found in existing texts.

■ Talk to colleagues who have taught the kind of course for which you are considering writing a text. Ask them to evaluate the existing texts for you. Ask them to describe the features that are most important in the kind of text you wish to write.

■ Obtain a few course syllabi from colleagues around the country to get an idea of the varied scope of the course as taught by different instructors.

■ Think of illustrations, tables, examples from everyday life, clinical examples, summaries, study guides, references, recommended readings, appendixes, glossaries, and indexes.

■ Think of a workbook, a coursebook, an instructor's manual, videotapes, audiotapes, test banks on computer disks, or other media products that might enhance the usefulness of your book.

■ Think of creative ways of organizing your book.

Write A Book Proposal

Write your book proposal after you have analyzed the market. Answer the following questions in your proposal:

1. What is your philosophy of the text and the subject matter on which you wish to write? Describe how you have taught the course or how you view the subject matter of the proposed text. What current and future trends are worth considering?
2. What is the title of your proposed book? Although the title may change, think of a brief title that directly suggests the content of the book.
3. What is the scope of this book? Who is the audience? Do you think the book may be useful to audiences other than students? Is this an undergraduate text? Graduate text? Dual-level text? (See Chapter 2 for a description of texts.) Suggest the courses for which the book may be a required or supplementary text.
4. What is the competition? Summarize the strengths and the weaknesses of the books on the market. Give the names of authors, titles of texts, years of publication, and the names of publishers of competing books.

5. What makes your book unique? How will it compete with the existing books? Your book may be unique because of comprehensiveness of coverage, easy and creative writing style, imaginative illustrations, and other unusual teaching devices. To maintain a competitive edge over existing books, include as many unique and useful features as possible.
6. What is the tentative table of contents? Give details on the organization of the book by suggesting all chapter headings and major subheadings.
7. How many pages do you expect to write? Estimate the number of typed double-spaced manuscript pages on letter size paper.
8. How many and what kind of illustrations do you plan to include?

Estimated number of line illustrations:
Estimated number of photographs:
Estimated number of tables:
Other illustrations (specify):

9. When do you expect to complete the manuscript? Or, from the date you sign a contract to write the book, how many months will you need to complete it? Please be realistic in your estimation so that the manuscript will be delivered on time.
10. What are your prior publications? Enclose your vita. Also, give details on other books you have written. Specify the dates of publication, price, and length of the books, the name of the publisher, number of editions published, and sales to date.

Appendix A includes an outline for writing a book proposal. Use that outline as it asks a few other questions as well. Send your book proposal to your publisher's in-house editor or a textbook series editor identified by the publisher.

■ IF YOU HAVE A COMPLETED MANUSCRIPT

Contact a Publishing House

If you have written some or all the chapters of a textbook, select a publisher to contact. First, find out who are the major textbook publishers in your discipline. There are many ways of finding a publisher who will accept your book, but initially, you should consider several.

You may think of publishers whose books you have used in your teaching. You may have met college representatives of publishing houses who often solicit manuscripts or book proposals from teaching faculty. Your colleagues, or colleagues who are published authors of textbooks, may suggest their publishers to you. You may know of a new or an established publishing house in your discipline that frequently markets texts to you and to other college faculty. You may know or have heard of a textbook series editor of a publishing company. You may have talked to an acquisitions editor in a publisher's exhibition booth at a state or national convention. These are among the important ways of finding information on publishers.

Select a few publishing houses initially. In making this selection, consider a few matters that are important for authors. Is the publishing house reputable? Talk to your colleagues to find out what they think of the publishing houses you have tentatively selected. Look at some of their publications. Do they publish the kind of product you plan to write? Are they of high quality? Have you used their books and other products in your teaching? If not, would you use them? How do they market their products to instructors and students? Do they spend money on direct marketing? (You know they do if you receive regular mailings from them.)

When you select one or more publishers for initial contact, make a phone call to an acquisitions editor at the publishing house. Describe what you have and ask if he or she would like to take a look at the manuscript. The interested editor will ask you to send either a few sample chapters or the entire manuscript with a cover letter. The editor also may ask you to prepare a book proposal of the kind outlined in Appendix A.

When one or more editors are interested in your book, you should find answers to additional questions before you make a final choice. Although the royalty contract you may negotiate is an important issue, there are other issues that are even more important. This is especially true for a new author or an author whose earlier publications were not successful. Publishers typically are skeptical about new authors as well as authors whose published books have been a commercial failure. These two kinds of authors have to sell themselves a bit harder than those who have published successful texts. Therefore, new or previously unsuccessful authors do not have much leverage in negotiating higher royalties. More importantly, such authors need stronger editorial help. Therefore, whether the publishing house provides strong and consistent editorial assistance is an overriding consideration for all but the most highly successful writers.

Ask the acquisitions editor about the publishing company's editorial process. Does the company have editorial consultants who will review your book proposal? Does it have a series editor who will work closely with you? Will the editor or editors work with you on organizing the content, coverage, and style of book? Will there be reviews of all chapters? Will they review revised versions of the manuscript as well? Will the editors send your chapters for expert reviews as well?

You will appreciate the editorial support you receive from the publishing house during the preparation of your manuscript. This support will make your writing experience efficient, productive, and enjoyable. In essence, a publishing house that your colleagues respect because it publishes high quality books, markets its products well, and provides good editorial support for its authors, should be your first choice. With such a choice, the new or previously unsuccessful author has a better chance of becoming successful. Successful authors always can negotiate better royalty contracts with their publishers.

Contact a Consulting or Series Editor

To find a publisher for your completed manuscript, you also may contact a consulting or series editor of a publishing house. The names of these editors usually are printed in texts they edit. The textbook directories or publicity materials also may contain the names of series editors.

A series editor, who usually is a faculty member in a university, may be your initial contact person. Series editors know the books in the series, the needs of the series, authors under contract, and books under preparation. The editor can answer most of the questions you should ask of any publishing house regarding editorial help, marketing, and so forth. If the editor is an experienced author and a respected colleague, you have found one good reason to select the publisher.

The series editor will discuss the feasibility of the proposed project. If in the judgment of the editor, the proposed project has merit and fits within the publication scheme of the publishing house, you will be asked to submit a book proposal and send parts or all of the manuscript. If the editor finds your manuscript acceptable, he or she will recommend it to the publisher.

2 Content and Organization of Textbooks

■ TYPES OF TEXTBOOKS

Textbooks may be classified as undergraduate, graduate, and dual-level. Although there are noteworthy differences among the three kinds of texts, they share many common characteristics.

Undergraduate texts are basic surveys of the field. In these texts, review of research and controversy are avoided or kept to a minimum. Terms, concepts, and methods are simplified as much as possible. Examples and illustrations are plentiful. Compared to a graduate text, the language and the writing style is less technical and the information covered is more basic.

Graduate texts offer an advanced review of a selected subject. Being more data-based than undergraduate texts, graduate texts include theories and controversies. These texts describe and evaluate important methodological issues and point out clinical or applied implications of theories and research data. Compared to undergraduate texts, graduate texts cover more territory and dive deeper into the subject. Well-written graduate texts may put on an impressive show of scholarship.

Dual-level texts are written for courses that are taught at either the advanced undergraduate or graduate level. In communicative disorders, for example, courses on stuttering, voice, laryngectomy, and statistics, among others, may be offered at either the graduate or advanced undergraduate level. Such courses tend to fall in between graduate and undergraduate courses. Instructors must give all the necessary information when their department does not offer another course on the subject. Therefore, dual-level texts written for such courses must combine the features of both graduate and undergraduate texts. They should provide basic information and review selected aspects of the subject matter at a higher level.

Although the three kinds of texts have unique features, they share many common characteristics. The following section describes some important characteristics of texts and points out the unique features of undergraduate, graduate, and dual-level texts.

■ CONTENT, ORGANIZATION, AND WRITING STYLE

It may be more difficult to write a successful undergraduate text than it is to write a graduate text. Dual-level texts are especially difficult to write. The problem is to gauge both the level and the amount of information instructors present in their courses at all levels of instruction. When you wish to write a text, you might examine several course outlines to assess the general scope of the course as it is taught across departments. After you have assessed the general scope and level of instruction, give some thought to the content, organization, and writing style you might use in your planned text. Then, write a book proposal using the outline given in Appendix A. The following suggestions will also help you shape your book proposal.

Texts as Teaching Tools

Unlike other kinds of books, **a textbook is a teaching tool**. If it is not written as one, instructors are not likely to adopt the book. Therefore, organize your text much like thoughtfully prepared classroom presentations. The more closely an instructor can follow your text in teaching a course, the greater the chances that the book will be adopted. Your textbook's orientation, organization, and content should be geared to the course as it is taught across most university departments.

In structuring the chapters of your text, consider the general organization of courses for which the book is intended. The text should present information in roughly the same logical sequence many instructors use. You need not strive to please every instructor, but a text in which information flows smoothly within a simplified and logically consistent structure is attractive to most instructors.

Comprehensive Coverage

Whenever possible, a text should serve as a single source of information for a typical course. Although graduate course instructors may require more than one text, most instructors of undergraduate courses are reluctant to do so. Many instructors at all levels of teaching are sensitive to the high cost of texts the students are required to buy. Therefore, to have a competitive edge over books that omit essential topics, make your text a comprehensive survey of topics included in a typical course.

Include important developments in the field that must be taught to students. Often, this information becomes the unique feature of a new text that competes with older, established texts.

Modular Writing

Sometimes it is not clear whether or not most instructors include a certain topic in their course. At other times, the author knows that some instructors include certain topics in their courses while others exclude the very same topics. In such cases, these topics become optional because they are not taught in each course on the subject. Include the optional topics in your text, but write them in a manner that allows them to be easily included by some instructors and just as easily excluded by others. Many instructors find a text with this type of *modular writing* more useful than those that omit important information.

To create modules of information, write optional topics in separate sections. Whenever possible, do not integrate optional information with mandatory information. Instructors can then assign or exclude separate sections that contain optional topics without affecting the integrity of other information.

Write a separate chapter on topics that are just emerging in the field that may be taught by an increasing number of instructors. If the available information is limited, then write them in distinct sections in a chapter.

Balanced Overview

All successful **texts are surveys**. Instructors who typically teach courses from their points of view reject texts that are heavily influenced by authors' personal views. Because it is the instructors holding varied views who make any text a success, it is important to give a balanced overview of the subject matter. This does not mean that textbook authors should sacrifice intellectual honesty. It means only that authors should show the same honesty in presenting all supported views, including their own. Combine an objective tone with your balanced coverage. Let your text reflect the current state of knowledge and practice, not just the views of some experts.

An **undergraduate text** may present different views in a simplified form. There is no need to cover controversies, arguments, and critical evaluations in depth. Avoid polemics, salesmanship, and inflated rhetoric in all texts. In an undergraduate text, do not include highly questionable "recent advances" that may be discarded before the book is published. Also, avoid viewpoints buried long ago.

A **graduate text** gives an advanced overview of a field and addresses controversial issues. Therefore, graduate texts should include important theories, their research bases, and methodological problems.

A **dual-level text** strikes a balance between undergraduate and graduate texts. Like an undergraduate text, it provides a basic survey of the selected field. Like a graduate text, it provides some advanced information. When a department offers only one course on a topic, instructors prefer to adopt texts with broad coverage of the subject matter.

When including advanced information in a dual-level text, be careful not to overwhelm the undergraduate student. The modular writing style described earlier is most suitable for dual-level texts. With this writing style, the more advanced information may be offered in separate chapters or sections.

Appropriate Content

The content of an undergraduate text must be simple, but not simplistic. Many scholars who have extensive writing experience know that it often is more difficult to simplify than to complicate matters. It requires extensive scholarship to present technical information simply and elegantly. The one who knows more can say less in a less cluttered or complicated manner. An instructor who talks big may be impressive, but texts that do the same make no impression at all.

The distinction between the simple and the simplistic is often difficult to draw, but many instructors do make that distinction. Thus, complicated and simplistic texts will meet the same fate. Determining the most appropriate level of content for a text at a given level of instruction is still a matter of judgment. Therefore, consult your colleagues and your editorial consultants. Study course outlines from several instructors as well as the contents of successful texts.

Unified Style in Co-authored Texts

Textbooks preferably are written by a single author. However, the complexity of certain subject matters may create a need for multiple authors.

If designed and written with care, texts written by two or three experts may be effective.

Co-authored texts need one lead author who will take the responsibility for the overall content and style of the text. Instructors will find a text with varying styles and uneven scope of chapters difficult to teach from. Students will find it harder to learn from. Therefore, the lead author of a co-authored text must ensure an even coverage of the material throughout the chapters. Each author should read the other authors' chapters and give feedback. Finally, the lead author should edit all the chapters to make sure that the styles are blended. As the student moves from one chapter to the next, there should not be distracting and contrasting styles. Smoothing out of stylistic differences is an important task of the lead author.

Even Style and Coverage in Edited Texts

Edited textbooks to which different experts contribute chapters often are unacceptable to undergraduate students and instructors. Such texts generally are better suited for advanced graduate courses, especially to doctoral seminars. Perhaps an acceptable exception is a text that describes contrasting methods of treatment, intervention, or teaching in which the author of each chapter is an expert on a particular method or approach. Another exception is a book devoted to advanced theories in which each author is a proponent of a theory. However, in all cases, edited textbooks require exceptional editorial efforts.

The editor of a textbook should have good knowledge of the topics, issues, theories, and methods each of the invited experts plans to write about. The editor should have the respect of all authors and be willing to ask for needed changes in chapters the other experts write. The clear lead role of the editor must be established from the beginning. From then on, the editor should be forthright with the authors. He or she should be tactful in dealing with the authors. The editor should be persuasive in effecting a smooth and even writing across chapters.

The editor and the contributors should agree on the general format, scope, content, and the writing style of all chapters of the edited book. The editor should enforce even coverage of the material to avoid the problem of some chapters being unduly detailed or excessively complex while other chapters are extremely scanty or overly simplistic. The editor and the authors should agree on the use of such features as the levels of heading, summaries, margin notes, clinical notes, boxed information, clinical case illustrations, bulleted or numbered lists, and study guides.

Then all authors should use the selected features and roughly to the same extent.

The editor should have the authors read each other's chapters. Thus, all authors will modify their content, orientation, and writing style to achieve a more unified presentation. A chapter that stands out from the rest because of its deficiencies needs special attention from both the author and the editor. A chapter with exceptionally favorable qualities will serve as a model for other authors.

The Use of Jargon

An important part of education is to teach students the meaning of technical terms and their correct usage. Yet, keeping the use of jargon to a minimum will enhance the appeal of an undergraduate text. Many topics may be described without jarring jargon.

Define the necessary technical terms simply but accurately. When something cannot be so defined, a simplified description is preferable. Long and windy definitions of already obscure terms are a great liability in all texts, especially in undergraduate texts.

Instructors expect graduate students to use technical language instead of lay language in their professional and scientific discussions. However, a major problem is that students studying a subject for the first time do not understand the meanings of technical terms. Therefore, define terms technically only after they have been defined nontechnically as well. Also, give an example from everyday life to illustrate a technical concept.

In later sections of the book, recapitulate abstract definitions discussed in the early chapters. To draw readers' attention to material presented earlier in the book, you may use margin notes, which will be described later in this chapter.

The Use of Illustrations and Examples

Good illustrations are important in all texts, especially in undergraduate texts. A few real-life photographs will make the text more realistic, but most textbook illustrations are either computer-generated or drawn by an artist. The more expensive artist-drawn or -prepared illustrations usually look better than those prepared on home computers. In addition, photographs of anatomical structures may enhance the students' understanding of the information presented.

Prepare clear and aesthetic illustrations. Anatomical illustrations need not be comprehensive, but they should depict the structural detail described in the text. Do not include structures that are not mentioned in the text in an illustration. When you use a schematic drawing, also show a picture or a more realistic illustration alongside of it.

Liberal use of interesting examples will promote a better understanding of difficult concepts. Examples provide a welcome break from a flow of technical information. In describing diseases and disorders, authors typically draw examples from clinical files, but illustrate general principles and concepts with examples from everyday life. Think of humorous or otherwise interesting examples to sustain the reader's interest.

The Use of Headings and Subheadings

Headings and subheadings should be planned thoughtfully. Different levels of headings (see Chapter 4) should help present the information in logical bits. In planning headings and subheadings, consider smooth transition and ease of understanding. If you prefer, number the chapter headings and subheadings consistently and systematically. On many word processors, these numbers will help automatically generate an accurate table of contents. You also can use the numbering system to reference portions of the text in which the student can find answers to study questions.

Undergraduate students find a liberal use of subheadings especially helpful. Information chunked by subheadings may be easier to grasp. Also, different subheadings may be clues for the students to remember different bits of information.

Use subheadings to simplify the writing and to prevent protracted and uninteresting discussions. In revising the manuscript, subheadings make it easier to delete or add information. However, keep the number of subheadings to a reasonable level. Too many subheadings may confuse the student by unnecessarily fracturing the information and destroying its continuity. Chapter 4 provides more information on designing headings and subheadings.

The Use of Section and Chapter Summaries

Students at all levels appreciate precise and thoughtful summaries. Undergraduate students especially need frequent summaries of technical information. Summaries can be valuable study aids in that the students can give them a quick glance before a test.

Write summaries at the end of major sections. Depending on the complexity of the subject, you may write shorter summaries at the end of subsections as well. Write a chapter summary at the end of each chapter. You may write summaries in paragraphs, boxed or table formats, or lists. You may devise other innovative ways of presenting summaries that stand apart from the text. Boxed summaries may be especially helpful at the end of major chapter headings. Summaries in lists may be appropriate at the end of certain major headings and subheadings. Chapter summaries generally are written in paragraphs, but here, too, your innovation will prevail.

You may suggest some way of setting the summaries off from the text so that they can easily be spotted in a quick glance of the text. Boxed summaries do best in this regard, but you may devise other graphic designs that are just as effective. For example, when summaries are written in lists consisting of single sentences, you may place a star or another icon at the beginning of each sentence.

The Use of Margin Notes

Margin notes are bits of information printed in the margins of a text. Use them to: (a) reiterate a short definition of a term given in a previous chapter, (b) give a piece of information not integrated with the text, (c) refer the student to another part of the book for a particular detail, and (d) give brief examples of concepts discussed in the text. You may find additional uses for margin notes.

Margin notes, like illustrations, help break a monotonous flow of technical information. But too many of them distract the reader from the text. Therefore, carefully consider the number and the kinds of margin notes to be included. Margin notes should be brief. They should supplement, not duplicate, the text.

To print margin notes, the printer should use a larger book size. Larger and unusual book sizes are more expensive to produce. Therefore, before you write margin notes, consult with your editors.

Study Guides

Study guides include questions to be answered, problems to be solved, and assignments to be completed. Study guides help students make a self-assessment of their understanding of the material. They are helpful in texts written for all levels of instruction. Typically, a study guide is written at the end of a chapter (before the reference list).

In certain texts, especially in undergraduate texts, you may write brief study guides at the end of major headings or sections of a chapter. Such sectional study guides help students assess their comprehension of smaller chunks of information that will promote a clearer understanding of subsequent sections of the chapter. Sectional study guides could discourage the student from proceeding to advanced sections of the chapter without a clear grasp of the preceding material.

Write unambiguous questions that test students' understanding of the material. Include various forms of questions to cover different instructors' styles of evaluation. Write multiple choice, true or false, fill-in-the-blanks, and short essay questions to assess student understanding of the material. Also, write questions that ask the student to define technical terms and to solve practical or theoretical problems. Include simulated situations for which the student must provide solutions that require integration and reflection of what is read.

Some instructors require their students to write answers to study questions. Therefore, provide enough space between questions to encourage students to write their answers. If practical, specify either the page number, the heading, or the subheading number that includes the information tested at the end of questions. This will make it easier for the student to reread the material and verify the answer.

Your publisher may print the study guide sections at the end of each chapter on perforated pages. If this is done, students can then tear out the answered guide and submit it to the instructor.

Recommended Readings

References cited in the text may be placed either at the end of chapters or at the end of the book. Because most undergraduate students are not likely to read them, give a list of recommended readings at the end of each chapter. This list should be short and include the choicest sources.

The books and articles recommended for further study should be appropriate for undergraduate students. When available, include literary works of interest. There are many autobiographical works written by recovered stroke patients who have had aphasia, individuals who stuttered or still do, recovered cancer patients, and parents of children with various disabilities and disorders. Several novels, stories, and children's books that sensitively portray people with communicative disorders, mental, behavioral, sensory, and physical disabilities are available. A few of these literary books and articles are listed in the bibliography. Students find the creative style and personal viewpoints of these books a refreshing alternative to professional books.

Quotations from literary works in the text tend to have dramatic effects on students. However, a word of caution in quoting from literary works is in order. Permission to reprint lengthy quotations from literary works is hard to obtain and usually involves undue delay. Also, most literary authors or their estates demand a fee, sometimes a considerable sum. Therefore, contact sources of intended quotations early to find out the feasibility and cost.

Portrayal of Clinical Populations

Texts in clinical disciplines portray people with various kinds of diseases, disorders, and disabilities. A rule in portraying people and their problems is to **put people first, not their problem**. Avoid the common tendency to identify people with their clinical labels. For example, instead of *A stutterer once told me . . .* write *An adult who stuttered once told me . . . . A child with cerebral palsy* is better than *A cerebral palsied child.* Similarly, *woman with arthritis, children who are deaf, adults with aphasia,* and *people with disabilities* are better than their often used counterparts (*arthritic woman, deaf children, aphasics,* and *disabled people*).

The pressure to be succinct sometimes makes it difficult to use less aversive but usually longer expressions. An alternative is to use such expressions as *disabled citizens, nondisabled people,* and *wheelchair user,* and so on. Never use such offensive expressions as *crippled, deformed, suffers from,* and *victims of.*

Nondiscriminatory Writing Styles

All texts must be written in nondiscriminatory language. The most common discriminatory style is the exclusive use of the male pronoun. Other kinds of writing styles that imply discrimination against a particular race, group, society, or culture also are prevalent. Many other expressions are stereotypes that suggest unfavorable evaluation of certain groups of people. Such evaluations are irrelevant to scientific and professional discussion. All expressions that imply or hint at discrimination and unfavorable evaluation against anyone must be scrupulously avoided.

When such a shift does not matter, use plural forms of pronouns to avoid an exclusive use of masculine or feminine pronouns. Revise *each child was asked to point to his nose,* to *the children were asked to point to their noses.* Or, use both the male and the female pronoun. The correct form is to write *he or she* (alternatively, *she or he*) but not "he/she" or "s/he." The sentences are a bit awkward when you use both the pronouns. To avoid this, alternate the use of *she* and *he.*

When referring to racial, cultural, and social groups, do not use language that suggest biases against them. Such references imply unnecessary and unjustified evaluation as well. The names of particular groups change over time. For example, the term *African Americans* is now preferred to the once-preferred word *blacks*. A general rule to follow is to select terms that members of particular groups use to refer to themselves.

Consult the *Publication Manual of the American Psychological Association,* Fourth Edition (1994), for more detailed suggestions on avoiding discriminatory language. A few other excellent publications on writing without bias are included in the bibliography.

Citation of References and the Reference List

Extensive citation of technical sources should be avoided in undergraduate texts. References to old and remote journal articles are unnecessary. For the undergraduate, recently published and readily available books are more practical than many journal articles. Reference to some classic, recent, or important journal articles may be necessary to document the research base of information presented. Still, in undergraduate texts, there should be no need to do this frequently.

Graduate texts that review vast amounts of research data tend to have longer reference lists. Even so, avoid the common tendency to inflate the reference list. Select references because of necessity, importance, and relevance to the discussion. Think of dropping a reference before you decide to include it.

Cite references in the text and arrange them in your reference list according to your publishing house's guidelines. A widely used format in behavioral sciences is that of the *Publication Manual of the American Psychological Association,* Fourth Edition (1994). There is more about this in Chapter 4.

Glossary and Index

Each text should have a glossary and a detailed and carefully prepared subject index. Some texts also have an author index. Only the author can prepare the glossary, but indexes may be prepared by either the author or a professional indexer hired by the publisher. The fee charged by the professional indexer is deducted from the author's royalties.

You may be the best person to prepare the index. You can make it as detailed and as discriminating as possible. You know the needs of the students; therefore, you can design your index so that it is most useful to them. Chapter 5 contains some suggestions on preparing an index.

Accompanying Coursebooks

A coursebook can enhance the usefulness of a textbook. A coursebook is a specialized teaching tool that accompanies a textbook. It defines all the important terms, lists major points, gives steps of treatment or other procedures, and thus reduces the burden of rapid note taking in the classroom. A coursebook also leaves the right half of each page blank so the student can write lecture notes on it. The student also may use a coursebook to take notes from additional readings. When properly used, a coursebook creates for the student a single source of information integrated from the text, class lectures, and additional readings. See Hegde (1994, 1996) for two examples of a coursebook.

Instructors, too, will find a coursebook useful for preparing for the classes. It provides a well-organized lecture outline already prepared for them. In the blank right-hand portions of each page, the instructor can write his or her own class notes. Generally, coursebooks make it a bit easier for the instructor to teach and for the student to learn.

A separate version of the instructor's coursebook also may be useful. This version will contain all the information in the student's version. In addition, the instructor's coursebook will have suggestions for special class assignments and complete tests or examinations along with answer keys. See Hegde (1995a, 1995c) for examples of instructor's and student's coursebooks accompanying a textbook (1995b).

■ SOME COMMON MISTAKES IN WRITING TEXTBOOKS

You write a textbook to facilitate teaching and learning of a subject. Some common mistakes in the design and writing of texts will defeat your purpose. You should carefully avoid these mistakes.

A primary mistake is to write a text exclusively for learned colleagues. A text is written simultaneously for colleagues who teach and students who learn. In designing your text, effective, clear, and simple communication is the primary target. Therefore, design and write a textbook for classroom instructors and their students.

Another primary mistake is to write a text as though it is a research monograph. A book that describes a line of investigation cannot be promoted as a textbook. Experiments and data are brought into a text occasionally, but only to illustrate or support major conclusions and summative statements. Also, the writing style of a textbook is less formal than that of a monograph.

Yet another mistake is to write texts to make critical reviews of research and data and to discuss controversial issues. Books devoted to doing this are not texts. They are specialized books that instructors and students often avoid. In a textbook, controversies are pointed out and briefly summarized, but rarely debated.

■ REFERENCES

Hegde, M. N. (1994). *A coursebook on aphasia and other neurogenic communicative disorders.* San Diego, CA: Singular Publishing Group.

Hegde, M. N. (1995a). *Instructor's coursebook for introduction to communicative disorders.* Austin, TX: PRO-ED.

Hegde, M. N. (1995b). *Introduction to communicative disorders* (2nd ed.). Austin, TX: PRO-ED.

Hegde, M. N. (1995c). *Student's coursebook for introduction to communicative disorders.* Austin, TX: PRO-ED.

Hegde, M. N. (1996). *A coursebook on language disorders in children.* San Diego, CA: Singular Publishing Group.

3 *Writing Style*

Authors of technical and professional textbooks are concerned with the accuracy and currency of information presented. Unfortunately, many authors of such books fail to pay much attention to writing style. Literary works thrive on their unique writing styles. Authors of fiction and stories, for example, come to be known for their unique styles cultivated with dedication and hard work. A pleasing style comes more easily to some authors than to others.

A pleasing writing style should be a goal of authors who write scientific, technical, and professional books. A textbook written in an easy and attractive style is more likely to be successful than the one written in a stiff, clumsy, and unimaginative style.

■ DEVELOP A UNIQUE STYLE OF WRITING

Technical writing can be pleasing if writers strive to develop a creative style of writing. Scientific and professional writers must discard the notion that constructing grammatically correct sentences is all that is required in good writing. Although suggestions will not ensure an attractive style, an author's persistent efforts to write in an interesting and creative style may eventually pay off.

To develop a creative writing style, think of new and interesting ways of expressing the same information. Study the established texts not only to find out what is good in them, but also to identify what has become a tiresome style. While writing, imagine teaching in the classroom. As an instructor, you have used novel methods of teaching. As a writer, you must devise similar, novel methods of saying, illustrating, and simplifying technical information.

Adopt a Simple Style

Write even advanced graduate texts in a simple style without sacrificing accuracy. A simple writing style is different from a content that is too low for a given level of instruction. Obviously, in graduate and dual-level texts you need to present complex levels of information, but simplify information to promote quick comprehension. Write in an uncluttered and elegant writing style that presents complex information at the student's level. Several popular writers of physical and biological sciences have set good examples in simple exposition of complex matters. Even lay readers can understand the subject.

To develop a simpler writing style, have persons not trained in your discipline or profession read and critique your writing. Constantly challenge yourself to simplify complex sentences and shorten longer ones. Express concepts more directly. If a shorter word will do the job, do not select a longer word. If a more common word says it more clearly, do not use an unfamiliar, ambiguous word. Do not constantly and unnecessarily drive your readers to their dictionaries. Most importantly, be convinced that only a good scholar and clear writer can simplify matters.

Write in a Lucid Style

Writing lucidly requires simplifying the subject matter to the judged level of instruction. A simple and attractive writing style is lucid. Lucidity also requires a smooth flow with easy transitions. Poor transitions often, but not always, are a result of not writing sentences that link paragraphs and sections of the book. A more troublesome reason for poor transitions is a confusing organization of topics within a chapter. Therefore, if it is difficult to make a transition from one topic to the next, consider a different alignment of topics.

Pay close attention to transition from paragraph to paragraph. To achieve a smooth transition, the first sentence in a new paragraph may relate to the idea expressed in the last sentence of the previous paragraph.

Limit the length of paragraphs to a few sentences expressing a unitary idea. Brief paragraphs are especially important in undergraduate texts. Three to four paragraphs a page may be ideal. A paragraph should never run longer than half a page. Longer, rambling paragraphs tend to mix information that is better separated in smaller and more easily grasped paragraphs.

Combined with an attractive style, lucidity and easy transitions between small paragraphs help carry the reader to the end. In addition, short, simple, and direct sentences and some humor may lighten the writing.

Eliminate Unnecessary Words and Phrases

To be precise and more effective, eliminate unnecessary words and phrases. Wordiness obscures meaning and asks the reader to make undue efforts to understand the writing. Many popular phrases clutter sentences and unnecessarily lengthen them as well. In most contexts, such phrases can be edited out completely or replaced with a single word. Consider a few examples:

Wordy	Eliminate or replace with
at the present time	now
at this point in time	now
question as to whether	whether
along the lines of	
as a matter of fact	
as far as . . . is (are) concerned	
by means of	
due to the fact that	because
for all intents and purposes	
hands-on experience	experience
in spite of the fact that	although
in the area of	in
in order to	to
is considered to be	is
on account of the fact that	because
the fact of the matter is	
the field of	just say *communicative disorders, chemistry, psychology*

until such time as	until
with regards to	
with respect to	
with reference to	
as of yet	yet
crisis situation	crisis
problem situation	problem
it seems to me that	(just say it)
a number of	several
it is certainly important to point out	(just point it out)

Avoid Redundant Phrases

Textbooks need some redundancy in information presentation. Major points need to be repeated and the same principle or concept may be described in different ways to promote understanding. Summaries repeat previously described material. This is acceptable redundancy. However, redundancy of terms is unnecessary. Avoid the following redundant terms and use the replacement as shown:

Redundant	**Essential**
future prospects	prospects
advance planning	planning
absolutely incomplete	incomplete
exactly identical	identical
repeat again	repeat *or* say again
each and every	each *or* every
totally unique	unique
uniquely one of a kind	one of a kind *or* unique
reality as it is	reality
actual (solid, true) facts	facts

famous and well-known	famous *or* well-known
goals and objectives	goals *or* objectives
three different kinds	three kinds
seven different varieties	seven varieties
four different types	four types
positive growth	growth
actively involved, actively looking	involved, looking
preconditions	conditions
unexpected surprise	surprise
successfully completed	completed
successfully avoided	avoided
necessary and essential	necessary *or* essential

Prefer Direct to Indirect Expressions

Excessively cautious and overly qualified writing is full of indirect and hedged expressions. Scientists and professionals wish to be cautious in making statements and careful about offering generalized statements. However, when these admirable qualities are carried to an extreme, writing becomes timid and meaning is obscured. Without overstepping the boundaries of careful writing and scientific restraint, a textbook writer should use direct expressions that convey unambiguous meaning. If a subject matter or issue is clouded or ambiguous because of conflicting results of research or limited knowledge, the writer should say so instead of drawing hedged and overly qualified conclusions. Students are especially confused by such writing.

Avoid using overly qualified phrases like *it certainly seems to me that, it is not entirely inappropriate to suggest that, it may be reasonable to assume that, it is certainly possible to assert,* and so forth. Just say what you want to say in terms that suggest the appropriate degree of certainty.

Maintain Parallelism

Express parallel ideas in the same grammatical form. Parallel forms are forceful and concise. Parallelism is broken when some ideas are expressed in one form and the other idea or ideas are expressed in a different form.

Nonparallel writing breaks the reader's expectation established by prior phrases. Parallelism is especially important in presenting information in numbered or bulleted lists and in describing steps to be taken in implementing a procedure. For example, if a list starts with a verb, *all* items in that list should start with a verb. If the initial parallel terms are nouns, the remaining initial terms also should be nouns. Consider the following examples:

Nonparallel	**Parallel**
Children with language disorders tend to be deficient in their use of grammatic morphemes, syntactic structures, and *they also may have problems in using pragmatic features.*	Children with language disorders tend to be deficient in their use of grammatic morphemes, syntactic structures, and pragmatic features.
Disadvantages of primary reinforcers include satiation, dietary restriction, and *they also are difficult to administer to groups.*	Disadvantages of primary reinforcers include satiation, dietary restriction, and problematic group administration.
In treating a child with autism, the clinician should:	In treating a child with autism, the clinician should:
• select objects as stimuli	• select objects as stimuli
• bring parents into the treatment sessions	• bring parents into the treatment sessions
• reinforce responses with tangible reinforcers	• reinforce responses with tangible reinforcers
• *be willing to* counsel parents	• counsel parents

■ FOLLOW THE STYLE OF THE PUBLISHING HOUSE

The term writing style has different meanings. A style is often the unique pattern of expression an author uses. However, the term style also means a specific set of publishing house guidelines to be followed in preparing a manuscript for publication. The term style in this sense includes many mechanical aspects of manuscript preparation.

When you sign a book contract, your publisher will send you detailed instructions on the style to be used. A *house style* is the format in which a publisher asks you to prepare your manuscript. A publishing house may have its own style or a style based on one of the widely used styles.

The house style for most of the textbooks published by Singular Publishing Group is based on the *Publication Manual of the American Psychological Association* (APA), Fourth Edition (1994). In some respects, the style recommended for authors of Singular textbooks does deviate from the APA style as described in the Manual's 4th edition. For example, the reference lists in Singular texts use the hanging indent (in which the second and subsequent lines of each entry are indented 3 spaces). Similarly, other publishing houses may modify better known styles. Therefore, you should be clear about the house style and strictly follow its guidelines. Following the guidelines from the beginning will save you revising time and effort. The editors will greatly appreciate your diligence in following the guidelines because it saves editorial time and effort as well.

The style of the American Psychological Association is widely used in many behavioral, social, and health-related sciences and professions. Thus, it is one of the standard styles used in the United States. Many scientific and professional organizations have their own standard styles. For example, the American Chemical Society, American Institute of Physics, American Mathematical Society, American Medical Association, Council of Biology Editors, and Modern Language Association have published styles. A classic and authoritative style used by many editors and authors is the *Chicago Manual of Style* published by the University of Chicago. Please see the bibliography for a list of these and several other style manuals.

Once again, study the style in which you need to prepare the manuscript for your publisher. Follow the guidelines from the beginning.

4 Preparation and Delivery of a Textbook

This chapter describes various mechanical aspects of text writing, including manuscript preparation and word processing the text. Selected portions of the *Publication Manual of the American Psychological Association*, Fourth Edition (1994), which should be followed in text preparation, also are included.

■ MANUSCRIPT DELIVERY DATE

To ensure timely publication of the text, deliver the manuscript on the date specified in the contract. If you expect problems in meeting the deadline, inform the sponsoring editor immediately. You and the publisher must agree on extensions. You should then make every effort to meet the new delivery date. Because the publisher makes production and marketing arrangements based on the manuscript delivery date, you should keep your promise.

Maintain an Efficient Writing Schedule

To complete their manuscripts on time, authors maintain different writing schedules that suit them the best. Authors who do not have a habitual writing schedule usually keep requesting additional time to finish their manuscripts. These authors write sporadically as the mood strikes them. They may not write for weeks or months, and suddenly, concerned about lack of progress, they will write a few pages. Feeling relieved, they stop writing and move on to other things. They do not write until they panic again. These are the authors who are tied to their projects for years and years.

You may already have a writing schedule that works for you. If you do not, establish one to meet the deadline for manuscript delivery. To be efficient, write every day, if possible, even if you do not write much on certain days. This helps keep the information alive in your head and will make most writing sessions productive. If a daily schedule is not practical, at least write on a few specified days of the week. On the days you plan to write, have a specific time to start. Eventually, certain days and times will prompt you to write.

Many authors think or talk about the amount of time spent on writing. Often, this only means the amount of time the author sat at the desk, which may or may not have been productive. To better self-monitor your writing behaviors, keep a continuous record of:

■ The cumulative number of pages written
■ The number of pages written in each writing session
■ The number of pages written per unit of time
■ The number of chapters or sections completed
■ The number of days left before the deadline
■ The amount of writing that remains to be done before the deadline
■ The amount of writing you can do in a week based on your past writing history

If you find yourself just sitting at the desk or at your computer terminal while your attention is wandering, get up and leave. Do something else for a short time, then come back to writing to see if the words begin to flow. Perhaps you did not have the necessary information at your fingertips to keep writing. Perhaps you needed to read and plan more. Regardless of the reason, sitting and staring at the paper or the computer monitor should not be habitual.

Make Scholarly Preparation for Writing

Lack of preparation is a reason for fruitless writing sessions. It is essential to have completed a review of scientific and professional literature before beginning to write. You need to establish a schedule for this as well. Let your reading schedule systematically precede the writing schedule. Take careful notes from your reading. Your writing will flow more easily if you write from your notes rather than from many articles and books spread around you.

Create a reference list of essential books and articles you are sure to cite in your writing. Keep the reference list on a separate document so you can copy and paste portions of it in the chapters you write. Add new citations to the reference list as you go along. Identify important quotations and keep them ready for insertion into your text. If you need to get some recent books, order them in advance.

Make photocopies of germane articles you plan to discuss in your writing. Prepare summaries of these articles and save them on a separate file. This will allow you to copy and paste relevant parts of summaries into your chapters.

Write From Chapter Outlines

Plan each chapter in detail. Prepare an outline of each chapter. A chapter outline contains all main headings and subheadings, including section and chapter summaries. The outline includes study guides, references if they will be placed at the end of each chapter, and recommended readings.

It is most efficient to have the chapter outlines prepared before you make specific notes for the various chapters. Your writing will be more efficient if you have entered your notes, thoughts, and information gathered from other sources under different headings and subheadings. Include major citations in your notes written under each heading. Then, write from this outline.

A carefully prepared and revised chapter outline reduces the chances of missing important topics or such pedagogical elements as section and chapter summaries. The outline and the notes it contains under headings will help evaluate the flow of text. You can judge whether topics are logically organized. If not, you can realign them by shifting the headings and subheadings. You also can evaluate whether the topics allow for smooth transition between sections. Select the type and number (levels) of headings. Once selected, use the headings and styles consistently throughout the book. Much editorial time and authors revision time are wasted when headings are not carefully thought-out and the levels used are confusing or inconsistent.

Various writing manuals including the *Publication Manual of the American Psychological Association* and the *Chicago Manual of Style*, both cited in the bibliography, give examples of various heading styles. Most word processors also contain default heading levels and styles. Word processors also have an outline feature that allows you to create chapter outlines with heading styles formatted. Default heading styles found in word processors fit most writing projects. Once created and stored as a formatted style, you can quickly and efficiently change the heading levels throughout the entire manuscript. An outline promotes a logically consistent flow of thoughts and information.

Print just the chapter outline with only headings and subheadings of each chapter (i.e., without your notes) and send it to the textbook series editor or the in-house editor for feedback. Use the editor's feedback to finalize the topics, headings, and subheadings. Writing after the structure of a chapter is finalized will result in more orderly writing of the first draft, easier editing, and therefore more efficient revisions.

See the section on headings in Chapter 4 for examples.

Get Started on Illustrations

Have a clear idea of the number and kinds of illustrations you will be using in the text. Hire an artist or create them on your computer. If you wish to use published illustrations, select them early in the writing process. **Always request signed permissions** (see Appendix B).

Supplying all illustrations and art work is an author's responsibility. Therefore, consider cost and efficiency in planning your illustrations. Before or as you start writing, have at least a rough version of illustrations ready. This will help you make appropriate references to them in your writing. Revising and editing books on anatomy and physiology can be extremely cumbersome if the illustrations are not incorporated in the early versions.

Seek Feedback on the Initial Drafts

Treat the writing of your first chapter as an experiment. However, try to write the first draft as tightly and elegantly as possible. Authors who push the philosophy of *cleaning it up later* to an extreme find that the revisions are both painful and endless. When working on a computer, periodically print out your writing and read it. Often, it is easier to find errors and organizational problems on a printed copy than on the computer screen.

Send the initial draft of your first chapter to your editor to get comments and suggestions. Have a colleague read and critique the chapter. Give it to a student and request comments. At this stage, do not be concerned too much about the finer points. The concerns include correct aim, smooth flowing organization, appropriate level of presentation, adequacy of coverage, clarity of writing, and effective communication. Consider such pedagogical devices as the number and length of margin notes, section and chapter summaries, figures and illustrations, and study guides. To avoid time consuming rewrites, do not write extensively before you settle on a style and an organization that suit the subject matter and the audience.

Revise the first chapter in light of the comments received. This time, make it as final as possible. Insert all illustrations in their appropriate places in the text. Send the revised chapter again to your editor. You probably will continue to write, but early feedback on a revised chapter will help you prepare the remaining chapters with greater finesse.

Write to publishing houses to get permission to quote from copyrighted sources as early as possible. Most publishing houses have forms you can use to request permissions (see Appendix B).

■ SUBMISSION OF THE COMPLETED MANUSCRIPT

Submit the original and two clear copies of the manuscript, including all tables, camera-ready illustrations, and permissions. Do not staple the manuscript pages; use rubber bands or heavy duty paper clips to hold them together. An author's checklist is provided in Appendix C.

Send the original art work at this time. Place the figures, photographs, and other art work in a separate envelope with stiff protective material to prevent bending. Pack the manuscript in a heavy-duty box and mail through the United Parcel Service (UPS) in the United States or equivalent form of registered mail. Keep two copies of your work, one at home and one at your office. This will be helpful if you have to discuss your manuscript with an editor while at home.

■ ELECTRONIC MANUSCRIPT PREPARATION

Today, most publishers require authors to prepare their texts on a computer. The ease and the speed with which manuscripts can be revised on a computer make the initial effort of learning to use a word processing program worthwhile. Also, books on computer disks can be produced faster, more accurately, and often less expensively.

Preparing Microcomputer Files of Text Chapters

Please use the following guidelines in your preparation of electronic files of your text chapters:

■ Prepare the files on an IBM or a 100% IBM-compatible computer or an Apple/Macintosh. The typesetter can then typeset your book directly off the disks. Typesetting from disks is faster, more accurate, and more economical than hand typesetting and reduces proofreading time.

■ Use the same word-processing program (e.g., Microsoft Word for Windows or Macintosh, WordPerfect for Windows or Macintosh) so that the typesetter can read your files easily.

■ Make separate files for each chapter. Place tables at the end of each chapter file or as separate files.

■ Use a grammar checker and a spell checker before you complete the manuscript. You may be pleasantly surprised at the amount of useful advice a good grammar checker can give. Spell check every section of a chapter each time you revise it.

■ Use the disk space efficiently, but do not overload disks. Each disk must have sufficient space for future editing. Also, please do not have files unrelated to the book or multiple versions of chapters on the disks submitted!

■ Output only contiguous chapters on a single disk (e.g., Chapters 1 and 2 on a disk, but not 1 and 5). Do not split a chapter between disks.

■ Enclose a printed copy of the table of contents. Check the contents and chapters one last time to make sure that chapter title, headings, and subheadings as shown in the table of contents are identical to those in the chapters.

■ On each disk, write the disk number and the total number of disks submitted (e.g., disk 2 of 5). Also, write an abbreviated title of your book, your name, the file names, the word-processing program (including the version) used or the system program version (for Apple/Macintosh), and the date. Finally, write "Press Copy" to indicate that the disk contains the final version of the manuscript. Keep in your possession copies of all disks submitted to the publisher similarly identified. Make sure that files on your disks and those sent to the publisher are identical.

■ The following are two disk label samples:

Example 1

Abbreviated book title
Disk 1 of 3
Linda Penn
Chapter 1, Chapter 2
Microsoft Word for Windows, version 6.0
10-8-96
Press Copy

Example 2

Abbreviated book title
Disk 1 of 4
John Wrider
Chapter 3, Chapter 4
WordPerfect version 6.0
Macintosh system program version 8
10-15-96
Press Copy

■ Ask your editor when the publishing house needs the disks. Some publishers need them during the editorial process; others may need them only after the manuscript is copyedited and the author has entered all the editorial changes on the disks. Most publishers handle only the printed copy during the editorial process.

■ In most cases, publishers will request the computer disks only when you have made all editorial changes and the book is ready for the typesetter. The disks submitted should not require any further text alteration.

■ When requested, send the disks with a copy of your printed manuscript. Make sure the printed copy is identical to the disk files.

■ Keep the original disks and backup copies. Send only a second set of backup disks each of which is labeled **Press Copy**. Again, make sure your original and backup disks contain the final version of the manuscript submitted to the publisher.

■ Mail the disks only in special disk mailers. Never use paper clips to attach a disk to anything.

■ Even if your disks are not 100% IBM compatible, submit them anyway. The files may be converted into a format the typesetter uses.

■ Avoid making hand-written changes in a word-processed text. In typed texts, enter unavoidable corrections in **black** or **red ink** only. Do not use blue ink because it does not register in scanning. Keep hand-written corrections to a minimum.

■ Please note that manuscript submission requirements change because of rapid technological advances. Therefore, always ask your publisher about current requirements.

Preparing Microcomputer Files of Art

Please use the following general guidelines in preparation of electronic files for illustrations. Always check with your publisher for more specific guidelines on artwork preparation because of rapidly changing computer technology.

- ■ Prepare all artwork files using either a 100% IBM-compatible computer or Apple/Macintosh computer.
- ■ Submit artwork on a separate disk or disks; do not combine artwork and text files.
- ■ Use a standard drawing program in preparing line art illustrations. If you plan to use a custom drawing program, check with your publisher to see if it can be used.
- ■ Save all artwork as EPS or TIFF files.
- ■ Save all line art files at 800 dpi. (Note: Even if your system cannot print at this resolution, the typesetter can and it will improve the quality of your printed illustrations. The typesetter *cannot* change your files to a higher resolution after they have been saved.)
- ■ Save photographic (halftones) files at 250 dpi. (Again, the typesetter cannot change your files to a higher resolution.)
- ■ Save all color files at 225 pixels.
- ■ Follow all other instructions for labeling and submitting text files on disk.

■ THE FINAL FORM OF THE MANUSCRIPT AT SUBMISSION

Arrange the manuscript in the following order before you submit it to the publisher.

Front Matter

Half title page
Title page
Contents page
All other preliminaries (foreword, preface, introduction, dedication, acknowledgments, etc.) that you plan to include
List of contributors and their addresses, if applicable

Text

Chapter title page, with complete names of contributors, if applicable
Text
Tables, on separate pages, placed at the end of chapter to which they apply (also double spaced)

Figure legends, on a separate page, placed at the end of the chapter to which they apply

Back Matter

References (double spaced, please!)
Glossary
Appendixes

The details of the front and back matter follow.

■ FRONT MATTER

Half Title Page

The half title page contains only the title and subtitle of the book.

Title Page

The title page contains the main title and subtitle of the book. On this page, list the names of authors or editors, their degrees, and their professional affiliations as you want them typeset. Include also, complete mailing addresses with the zip code and telephone, fax, and e-mail numbers for each author.

Contents Page

Ensure that the contents page is accurate and matches the chapter opening pages. In edited books, the chapter titles and the names of the contributors should be the same in both places.

Beyond the chapter headings, the contents page may include first level headings of each chapter. Do not include secondary and subsequent headings on the contents page.

Foreword

Someone other than the author or the editor of the book writes a foreword. Typically, a recognized authority in the field writes an overview of the subject matter of the book that may serve to highlight its importance or historical significance. A foreword is signed by its author and generally runs about two to four manuscript pages.

A foreword is optional in textbooks. It is typically solicited by the author. If you wish to have someone write a foreword for your book, discuss it with your editor.

Preface

The author or the editor writes a preface. It is typically three to six manuscript pages in length and is unsigned. A preface describes the author's purpose in writing the book and offers a summary of each chapter. The preface describes the unique characteristics of the book, the need for it, and why readers should read it. It also defines the book's audience.

The preface also may be used to clarify unusual content, style, spelling, or organization of the book. Every text must have a preface.

List of Contributors

For multicontributed books, prepare two lists of contributors. The first list should include the names of the editor(s) and authors, their degrees, and institutional affiliations. This information will appear in the book. The second list should include names, mailing addresses, telephone and fax numbers, and e-mail addresses of all contributors. Include zip codes. Double check the accuracy and currency of information on each list. Arrange the two lists alphabetically according to last name. The publisher will use the second list for correspondence with the contributors.

Acknowledgments

In the final paragraph of a preface, the author or the editor may acknowledge substantial help received from individuals. If you have many individuals, organizations, and corporations to acknowledge, type the names on a separate page headed "Acknowledgments."

Dedication

Type the dedication, if you choose to include one, on a separate page. Avoid ornate or sentimental language in writing your dedication.

Introduction

A short and general introduction can be a part of the preface itself. When a preface is not sufficient, write an introduction. Although longer than a preface, an introduction should not be of chapter length.

If you need a lengthy introduction to the total subject matter covered by the chapters, write it as the first chapter of the text. It will then be an introductory chapter but will not be headed "Introduction." If needed, write a historical overview of the subject matter as a separate (introductory) chapter.

■ BODY OF THE TEXT

Typing or Computer Printing

Spacing, Margins, and Lines

Do not use single spacing or one-and-a-half spacing in any part of the manuscript. **Double space the entire manuscript**, including the title page, headings of all levels, the text, quotations, tables, figure legends, and reference lists. Use triple spacing before starting a major heading or before and after a blocked quotation.

The **margins** should be 1½ inches (4 cm) on the top, bottom, right, and left of every page. The editors and the copy editors need the margin space to make editorial remarks. Consistent margins throughout the text and on all four sides of each page also help editors to accurately estimate the length of the printed book.

Do not hyphenate words at the end of a line. On some laser printers this cannot be avoided even when right justification is not used. Other computer printers or word processing programs automatically avoid hyphenated words.

Do not use right justification when using a computer printer. When not justified, the right margin will be uneven. Right justification results in an even right margin but uneven space between words. This makes the manuscript difficult to read. Also, typesetting will involve additional time to delete the extra spaces between words.

Acceptable Typefaces

Print your manuscript on a **letter quality** or **laser printer**. No matter how fine the quality, do not use dot matrix printers as they create problems when the original manuscript is duplicated for reviewers and typesetters.

Computer printers, especially laser printers, offer many typefaces and pitch points. Whether you use a typewriter or a computer printer, select a typeface that is easy to read. Avoid exotic and excessively ornamental typefaces that are difficult to read. The pitch and the point size of the letters should not be too small or too big; sizes between 10 to 12 may be appropriate. Use the larger size for headings and subheadings. Use the same typeface throughout the text. Do not use condensed type in any portion of the text. Use boldface type only for headings or to highlight technical or other important terms that are defined.

Paper

Use 8½ × 11 inch white, nonerasable, unlined bond paper. Do not use inferior quality papers that tear easily in shipping and handling.

Page Numbers and Page Heading

Number all pages of the manuscript consecutively, including tables and other end materials. An *exception: do not number the pages that contain figures and figure captions.* Insert these unnumbered pages at the end of each corresponding chapter following all numbered material.

Most word-processing programs allow you to print page numbers automatically on each page. Page numbers should be placed at the top right-hand corner of the page, either below or five spaces to the right of the page header. Print the page header, if used, at the top left-hand corner of each page.

When you delete or add pages, renumber or repaginate the entire chapter. Avoid the common practice of giving a new identity to the inserted page (e.g., 7A, 25B).

Do not print your name on any page of the manuscript. It should appear only on the title page which will be removed if the manuscript must be blind-reviewed.

Corrections

There is no need to have hand-written corrections on the manuscript when the text is word-processed. Corrected pages are easily and quickly reprinted. Even when the manuscript is hand-typed, corrections should be few. Do not use correction paper or liquid; retype corrections. Corrected words and lines should be in their proper space and not in the margins. Do not paste or tape slips of papers containing corrections to the manuscript pages. Retype a corrected page that looks messy as it may confuse reviewers and editors. Again, ensure that the final version of the manuscript (printed copy) is identical to the documents on the disks.

Indentation and Spacing

Indent the first line of each paragraph of the text five spaces. But do not indent the following:

■ The first line of the first paragraph under a heading or subheading
■ Block quotations
■ Titles and headings, titles of tables, and legends of figures
■ The first line of each reference in the reference list (see References for additional guidelines)

Leave only **one space** at the end of sentences (following periods). Use one space after commas and semicolons.

■ CHAPTER ORGANIZATION

Give some thought to how you want to organize each chapter of the book. First create a sample chapter outline, which serves as the skeletal structure that you later fill in with text. You will have created preliminary chapter outlines when you submitted your book proposal. However, these early outlines are almost always changed.

When you are ready to write the chapters, you should finalize the structure of each chapter. Changes are fine assuming that the book does not take a radically different shape than the one you signed a contract for. If you wish to make significant changes in the chapter outline, and hence the content of the book, discuss the matter with your sponsoring editor, your textbook editor, or both.

Your chapter structure should contain everything you wish to include. Among other elements that may be unique to a particular book, the structure should include the following:

■ headings and subheadings
■ levels of headings and their style
■ number of figures and illustrations
■ margin notes
■ clinical or application notes
■ historical notes
■ case or experimental illustrations
■ boxed entries or stories
■ section and chapter summaries
■ study guide
■ practice sheets, lessons, and other materials of this nature
■ references and suggested readings

As suggested earlier, it is most efficient to create a chapter outline and a style for the particular book on your computer. Major word-processing programs allow you to create a style and give it a name, such as the name of the text itself. A style would include paragraph formats, fonts and their sizes, heading styles, reference formats, and so forth. As you begin a new chapter, you can automatically apply the style of the book to it. This way, your chapters will have an identical structure.

Chapter Title

Each chapter should begin on a new page with the chapter title printed in boldface. You may or may not begin the text on this first page. In any case, it is desirable to give the major (level 1) headings in bulleted form on the first page of each chapter.

Give your chapters simple, short, and direct titles. Repeat the title and the number of the chapter on every page. Use the header function in word processors to do that. Print the title on the left-hand side of the page and print the page number on the right side, justified.

Headings

Pay careful attention to headings within chapters. Headings should be brief and direct. A heading should normally occur every four to six pages. In an undergraduate text use headings and subheadings liberally. Each chapter will start with an introduction, which usually is untitled, because it is obvious from its placement in the chapter.

Three to four levels of headings (also called "weights") usually are adequate for most textbooks. The following are examples of three and four levels of headings and their suggested styles that could be used consistently; all headings are printed in boldface:

Example of Three Levels of Headings

THIS IS A LEVEL 1 HEADING

Capitalize all letters and center the level 1 heading.

This is a Level 2 Heading

Capitalize the important words of the level 2 heading. Type it flush left.

This is a Level 3 Heading.   Indent the level 3 heading as for a paragraph. After two spaces, start the text on the same line like this; type the heading in upper- and lowercase letters; capitalize the important words; and italicize it. This is the only heading that ends with a period.

Example of Four Levels of Headings

THIS IS A LEVEL 1 HEADING

Capitalize all letters and center the level 1 heading.

This is a Level 2 Heading

Center the level 2 heading. Use the upper- and lowercase letters; capitalize the important words.

This is a Level 3 Heading

Type flush left the level 3 heading. Use upper- and lowercase letters; capitalize important words.

    This is a Level 4 Heading.   Indent the level 4 heading as for a paragraph. After two spaces, start the text on the same line like this; type the heading in upper- and lowercase letters; capitalize the important words; and italicize it. This is the only heading that ends with a period.

Note that under most headings, the first paragraph is typed flush left. The second and subsequent paragraphs are indented by 5 spaces.

Throughout your manuscript, use the selected levels of headings consistently. Do not mix different typefaces; use a single typeface for the text and the headings.

Quotations

Do not use too many quotations in texts. Select a few quotations that say something superbly and make a lasting impression on readers. Memorable quotations are typically short, whereas lengthy quotations are often soon forgotten.

Quotations cited in a text must be faithful to the original wording. Make sure that quotations are identical to the original in words, spelling, and punctuation. Reproduce errors as they are in the original with the insertion of the word [sic], underlined, and placed within brackets as shown in the example:

Example 1

Numbasa's description of language as a mental phenomenon "that can be studied only by some powerfil [sic] intuitive procedures" (1971, p. 57) was especially appealing to clinicians who had based treatment procedures on their own intuition.

Quotations of less than 40 words should be integrated as part of the text and enclosed within **double quotation marks**, as shown in the following example:

Example 2

Numbasa (1971) defined language as "A cognitive ability to synthesize and symbolize mental experience and to represent this experience in patterns of sounds, words, and sentences following linguistic rules that are innately given" (p. 95). This definition of language became instantly popular with linguists and cognitive psychologists.

Use single quotation marks to separate one quotation within another; in the original, this would have been enclosed within double quotation marks:

Example 3

Numbasa (1971) stated that it is "important to study this 'mental' experience to fully understand language and its function" (p. 97).

In example 3, the word "mental" was placed within double quotation marks in the original. The author who quoted Numbasa placed the word within single quotation marks because it is within the double quotation marks.

Punctuation marks associated with a quotation depend on how the quotation is begun and ended. Generally, periods or commas are placed within the closing quotation marks; other punctuation marks are placed outside the quotation marks. But this, too, depends on how the quotation is integrated into the text:

Example 4

The strong phonological theory claims that "acquisition of sound patterns is regulated by some universal principles" (Snuff, 1980, p. 56).

Example 5

Numbasa's theory stated that language acquisition is "complex beyond imagination and hence is not subjected to methods of empirical investigation" (1971, p. 35).

Example 6

Numbasa (1971) stated that "language as we define it is not a product of evolutionary changes" (p. 78).

Note that when a sentence is ended with a quotation and at the end of it, either the page number, year and page number, or the author's name, year, and page number are typed within parentheses, the period is typed after the closing parenthesis.

However, when the quotation is ended without the author's name, year of publication, or the page number, the period is placed within the closing quotation marks.

Example 7

Bluff (1996, p. 279) stated that "Stuttering is not the same as speech interruptions that all normal speakers exhibit."

When a quotation is in midsentence, and the year of publication and the page number within parentheses are typed at the end of the closing quotation marks, type a comma after the closing parenthesis and continue the sentence.

Example 8

Bluff stated that "stuttering cannot be measured by merely counting the number of dysfluencies" (1996, p. 230), though he did not specify how it should be measured.

Quotations that exceed 40 words must be set apart from the text as a **block quotation**. Add an extra line (triple space) before and after a block quotation. Indent five spaces from the left margin and type a block quotation to conform to the new margin. No quotation marks are necessary for block quotations. However, a quotation within a block quotation must be placed within double quotation marks. After the quotation, type the page number of the quotation within parentheses as shown in the example:

Example 9

In his landmark book on language intervention, Mumbasa (1991) revealed the nature of language intervention:

Language intervention is a process of unleashing powerful but painfully hidden though unconsciously active communicative potential. The goals of language intervention include transcendental self-actualization, realization of mental potential, and remodeling of perceptual-emotive reality. These goals are most successfully met by forging a unity between the unknown demands made on the individual and his or her hidden but striving communicative potential.

> If the process of language intervention as described in this book sounds mysterious, it is because the process is mysterious. A successful clinician has an innate ability to solve this mystery. (p. 997)

Mumbasas compelling views on language intervention influenced many clinicians who believed that many experts who unsuccessfully tried to use the scientific methods had trivialized the intervention process.

Note that in the example of a block quotation, there are no quotation marks at the beginning and the end. The text of the quotation ends with a sentence but there is no period after the closing parenthesis. In the typed manuscript, one space is given before the first parenthesis is started to enclose the page number. The first line of the subsequent paragraphs of a block quotation is indented five more spaces as shown.

Changed Quotations

Any change you make to a quotation should be apparent to the reader. Insert three ellipsis marks (...) to show that you have omitted words from a quoted sentence. Insert four ellipsis (....) points to indicate you have omitted words between any two sentences. Give a space before and after each ellipsis point. Generally, ellipsis marks are not necessary at the beginning and end of a quotation even when it begins or ends in midsentence. If words have been inserted into a quotation, enclose them within brackets.

Underline or italicize the words you emphasize that were not emphasized in the original source. In either case, type the words [italics added] within brackets after the underlined or italicized words. Note that the typesetter automatically italicizes all underlined words. If for some reason, you want certain words underlined, underline them and handwrite "underline, do not italicize" in the margin of the printed text.

Abbreviations

Frequent use of abbreviations hinders clear understanding of the material. The students, not being familiar with the terms, tend to have difficulty remembering the meaning of abbreviations that are spelled out somewhere in the book. Therefore, write out all technical abbreviations the first time they are used in *each* chapter.

Do not start a sentence with a lowercase abbreviation. Although uppercase abbreviations may start a sentence, it is better to avoid them as well.

Write out abbreviations of technical words or other terms the first time they are used and enclose the abbreviation in parentheses:

■ American Speech-Language-Hearing Association (ASHA)
■ Average Daily Attendance (ADA)
■ Before meals (a.c.)
■ Certificate of Clinical Competence (CCC)
■ Chronological Age (CA)
■ Conditioned stimulus (CS)
■ Consonant-vowel-consonant (CVC)
■ Cerebrovascular accident (CVA)
■ Decibel (dB)
■ Developmentally Disabled (DD)
■ hearing threshold level (HTL)
■ Hertz (Hz)
■ Mean length of utterance (MLU)
■ temporomandibular joint (TMJ)
■ Three times a day (t.i.d)

Subsequently, use only the abbreviation except at the beginning of a sentence. **Do not write out words** for the following commonly used abbreviations:

■ Units of time: sec, min, hr.
■ Units of measurement when accompanied by a number: 20 kg, 5 cm, 115 lb, 29%.

Write out the units of measurement when a number is not specified:

■ the weight was specified in kilograms
■ measured in centimeters
■ several pounds of sugar
■ percentages of dysfluencies

Type abbreviated units of measures **without a period at the end**:

■ cm, kg, cd, sec, ft, lb

Note the **two exceptions**:

■ The word inch, when abbreviated, takes a period (in.).
■ All abbreviations take a period when they appear at the end of a sentence.

Never use plurals with abbreviated units of measurement:

- 5 hr (not 5 hrs.)
- 10 cm

Always **write out** the following:

- day(s)
- month(s)
- week(s)
- year(s)
- inch(es)
- liter
- foot (feet)
- micrometer (not micron)

Add the plural morpheme *s* to plural abbreviations; do not add an apostrophe:

- ABRs; ECGs; EEGs; IQs; Eds.; vols.

Add periods to the following:
- initials of names (Q. T. Quinn)
- geographic names (U.S. Military)
- U.S. as an adjective (U.S. Department of Health and Human Services)
- Latin abbreviations: i.e.; vs.; a.m.; e.g.
- reference abbreviations: vol.; 2nd ed.; p. 10.

Do not add periods to the following:

- capital letter abbreviations and acronyms: ASHA; APA; NIH, UNESCO; IQ.
- abbreviations of state names

Do not abbreviate "United States" when it occurs alone as a noun in text.

Use the following **Latin abbreviations** only within parentheses; in running text, use their English equivalents:

(i.e.,)	that is
(cf.)	compare
(viz.,)	namely,
(etc.)	and so forth
(vs.)	versus

Exception: Use the abbreviation *v.* (underlined or italicized) in references and text citation to court cases in both parenthetical and nonparenthetical writing.

Examples

Certain variables, **namely**, intelligence, personality, and socioeconomic status are known to . . . (Nonparenthetical construction)

Certain variables (**viz.**, intelligence, personality, and socioeconomic status) are known to . . . (Parenthetical construction)

The severity of hearing loss, the type of loss, the age of onset **and so forth** are known to . . . (Nonparenthetical construction)

Many factors (severity of loss, type of loss, the age of onset, **etc.**) are known to . . . (Parenthetical construction)

It is cumbersome to read sentences that are full of these Latin abbreviations. Overuse of even the English equivalents of *i.e.* and *viz.* make the reading difficult. Try to avoid their use:

Intelligence, personality, socioeconomic status, and other variables are known to . . .

Factors including the severity of loss, type of loss, and the age of onset are known to . . .

Seriation

Use **serial comma** before *and* and *or:*

Every woman, man, and child in the country

As shown in a study by Tent, Bent, and Lent (1990)

The age of onset, the level of hearing loss, or the type of loss

To separate series that have within-series commas, use **semicolons:**

The order of presentation was one, two, three; three, two, one; or, two, three, one.

(Beans, 1989; Cane & Stone, 1990).

To separate series within a paragraph or sentence, use **lowercase letters** within parentheses and without underlining:

At the end of the session, the child could select either (a) a toy to play with, (b) a book to read, or (c) a scoop of ice cream to eat.

However, if sentences that describe a series have internal commas, separate the series with semicolons:

During the session, the child was asked to (a) point to a household object, picture, or toy; and (b) name the object, picture, or toy.

Use of Numbers

Use **roman numerals** only when it is an established practice:

Cranial nerve IV

Type II error

Use **arabic numerals** for all numbers 10 or higher:

11 tests

25 students

150 patients

Note that unless they start a sentence, the first letter of the words *roman, arabic,* or *india* ink is **not capitalized**.

Exceptions:

1. Always use arabic numerals with units of measurement even when the units are below ten:

   6 dB, 3 min, 5 years

2. When numbers are used in series and some are less than 10 and some are more than 10, use all numerals:

   This was found in 5 of 21 subjects.

   There were similar findings in 5 cats, 6 rabbits, and 13 dogs.

Write Out in Words:

1. A number at the beginning of a sentence:

   Twenty-five students took 11 tests.

Eighty percent of patients with aphasia improved with treatment while 20% showed no change.

2. Numbers below 10 that are not precisely measured values and are not grouped for comparison with numbers 10 and above:

four to six words
two treatment sessions
seven pages
three test items
nine morphological features
eight dysfluencies
one-tailed *t* test

Use of Zero

Use zero before a decimal point:

0.47, not .47

Do *not* use zero to show probability levels or correlations:

r: + .78; *p* < .01

Plural Forms of Numbers

Add the grammatic morpheme (*s* or *es*) to a numeral or word, but do not use an apostrophe:

1960s and 1970s

10s and 20s

sixes and eights

Use of Metric System

Use the metric system to report all measurements. If it is necessary for quick comprehension, give the nonmetric equivalents in parentheses.

Use of Phonetic Symbols

When you use International Phonetic Symbols, list all symbols used in the text on a separate page. This summary sheet is necessary to ensure the accuracy in the presentation of phonetic symbols in the text.

Clearly and accurately handwrite the phonetic symbols that you cannot type or print. In undergraduate texts for courses typically taken before phonetics courses, it may be prudent not to use too many phonetic symbols. In a few initial places, describe the sound with the traditional orthography and give an example of a common word with the phonetic symbols (e.g., / θ / voiceless *th* as in *think*).

On the summary sheet, show all allophones, diphthongs, diacritical marks, and any other symbols used in the text. Make a photocopy of typeset symbols or diacritical marks from an already printed source and enclose it for comparison.

Equations and Displays

Type small equations on line in the text: $a = 2 \times (b + x)/1$. Display complex equations that do not fit within the line on a line set off by at least four spaces from the text.

Identify all **Greek letters** and symbols in the margins using black or red ink. Equations referred to later in the text should be numbered by placing an arabic numeral in parentheses at the right-hand margin. In subsequent references, refer to the equation by the number, but without the parentheses (e.g., "As shown in equation 1, the values . . .). Underline all letters that refer to mathematical values so they may be set in italics.

Tables

Consider carefully the use of tables to present information in textbooks. In journals, tables typically contain quantitative data. However, in textbooks, tables also may contain text (words) to summarize an area of investigation or provide qualitative information. Summaries of speech or language development in children, for example, may be presented in tables.

In undergraduate texts, do not present complicated and lengthy quantitative data. Use tables to simplify information and save space by avoiding extended discussions in the text. Design simple, elegant, and graphically appealing tables.

When you use tables to present a general summary of information on a given topic, discuss the topic only briefly or just refer the student to the table. Use small tables after different sections of a chapter to summarize what is said in those sections. Tables that are not summaries of sections of a chapter should supplement, not duplicate, the text.

In designing tables, use only horizontal lines, and keep them to a minimum. *Never use vertical lines* and *do not use shading or screens.* Each column must have a heading. These headings at the top of a column, known as boxheads, should be brief and to the point. If they should contain some units of measurement, enclose them in parentheses.

Make sure each quantitative table you design can fit on a printed page. Although tables containing words can run more than a page, it is still desirable to keep them as short as possible. Try to avoid tables that must be printed sideways on the page because such tables are not read easily.

Each table should have a succinct title that captures the essence of its contents. Use a consistent set of symbols throughout the book to identify table notes. For example, a lowercase lettering system is easily understood and is recommended. In the note, clearly explain each symbol used in the table. Type these notes below the bottom rule of the table. Place source acknowledgments, if any, in a separate paragraph under the table as an unlettered table note. Write the full citation.

Within a chapter, number tables consecutively with arabic numerals. The first numeral should stand for the chapter number and the second for the chronological order of the table within the chapter (e.g., Table 2-6 for the sixth table in the second chapter). Do not design a combined system of numerals and letters of the alphabet (1, 1a, 1b). Cite all tables in the text by their number (Table 1-5, Table 7-9, etc.). Each table will be placed following its initial citation in the text. Do not cite tables at the end of sections to avoid the problem of tables falling on a page or two away from the relevant text.

Do not refer to tables with such phrases as "the table below," "the table above," or "the table on page 189" because the spatial relation between the text and tables will vary when the final book pages are composed. An example of a table follows:

Example of a table

Table 5-1. The types and frequency of dysfluencies exhibited by the subjects.

Subjects	Types of Dysfluencies					
	PWR	**WWR**	**PRO1**	**PRO2**	**INT**	**BW**
1	7	13	8	5	12	3
2	11	18	9	7	22	10
3	18	12	16	14	10	5
4	8	6	9	11	17	7
5	9	10	15	13	16	4

Note: PWR = part-word repetitions; WWR = whole word repetitions; PRO1 = sound prolongations; PRO2 = silent prolongations; INT = interjections; BW = broken words.

Source: From "Patterns of dysfluencies in young children" by Z. D. Twist and B. Z. Nest, 1991, *Journal of Dysfluencies, 20*, p. 28. Copyright 1991, by Kiran Publishing Company. Reprinted (or Adapted) by permission.

Below is an example of credit given to a book from which a table was reprinted:

> *Source*: From *Introduction to stuttering* (4th ed.), (p. 235) by T. Stetson, 1996, Dinkytown, CA: Sail Smooth Publishing. Copyright 1995 by Sail Smooth Publishing. Reprinted by permission.

Figures

All illustrations, excluding tables, are called figures. Like tables, figures should not duplicate the text. Figures should augment the text, illuminate relations that are better shown graphically, and help avoid lengthy discussions.

Design simple and aesthetically pleasing figures. In a figure, do not include unnecessary details or material not mentioned in the text. Make sure your figures suit the intended level of instruction. Use a consistent format for all figures in the book. Use a sans serif typeface for all text in figures (e.g., Helvetica, Univers).

There are various types of illustrations including graphs, charts, diagrams, drawings, maps, and photographs. Imaginative authors can devise other kinds of illustrations that simplify the teaching material. Most of these illustrations fall into two categories: photographs and line art.

Photographs

Good photographs are eye-catching. Photographs of people are especially appealing to students. Therefore, consider including a few photographs in your text. Note that high-quality black and white photographs are especially difficult to take. Therefore, hire a professional photographer who specializes in black and white photography.

1. Submit black and white glossy photographs only. Pictures should have a dark background that provides good contrast without shadows. Retouching is not acceptable.
2. On the back of each glossy, attach a gummed label on which the name of the book author or editor, figure and chapter number (e.g., Figure 2-1), and chapter author (if applicable) are written. Write TOP to suggest the correct orientation of the picture. **Do not write in pen or pencil directly on the back or front of photographs** to prevent indentations or potential ink smears.

3. Never incorporate figure captions into the photographs. Legends identifying symbols in the photograph, however, must be included.
4. Do not submit a photograph of a photograph because it will not reproduce well. Therefore, when you wish to borrow a picture from another source, request the original from the publisher.
5. Submit the original photographs with the initial submission of your manuscript. Before you take many pictures, send a few original photographs to the in-house editor to find out if they are acceptable.
6. Put pictures for each chapter in an envelope and place them at the end of each chapter. Do not use staples or paper clips to hold pictures together. Do not attach photographs to anything.

Line Art

Line art illustrations are made with black lines and include simple drawings, diagrams, and bar and line graphs. An author who is not skillful in preparing illustrations should hire a professional artist. Line art may be prepared manually or using one of the many computer drawing programs available today.

1. In preparing line art manually, use black indelible ink such as india ink. Draw the figures on white bond paper to enhance the contrast. Do not place ordinary handwritten or typewritten letters on the figure, except those that can be typeset. All letters that are reproduced (not typeset) must be simple and dark. The letters should have clear bold lines that retain legibility when reduced or enlarged to half their original size. Use upper- and lowercase letters. All-capital letters are hard to read.
2. Design illustrations that are no larger than the size of a printed page. The quality of the final print may be affected when the typesetter reduces larger figures (e.g., photo reduction reduces spaces between dots in halftone screens, making them darker, and small original type or fine line art also may become unreadable). Preferably, design rectangular artwork so it can be adapted to a book page. While not sacrificing clarity, keep the size of your figures small so they can be easily placed in the right place in the text. Students can then read the text and look at the illustrations more readily than when the illustrations are placed away from their text citation as is often the case with large illustrations.

3. Draw graphs and charts on white bond paper. Make sure that the vertical axis is two thirds the length of the horizontal axis. Correctly label the two axes of the graph. Plot the dependent variable on the vertical axis and the independent variable on the horizontal axis. Do *not* label the vertical axes vertically. Specify the units of measurements on carefully selected grid scales. Use sharp looking geometric forms to distinguish one line or bar from the other. Let the design be simple and clear. Use no more than four lines in a line graph.

4. Prepare illustrations, especially graphs and charts, on your computer with graphic, paint, and draw programs. However, most illustrations initially generated by such programs are not of high quality. The lines are often thin and broken. Good looking rounded illustrations are especially difficult to produce. Many software programs allow you to modify such illustrations on the computer screen to turn them into camera-ready quality. Print computer-generated illustrations on a high quality (600 dpi) laser printer. **Never print the final version of illustrations on a dot matrix printer**. These are unacceptable and will not be redrawn. If you do not have access to a high quality laser printer, have a copy shop or a graphic design shop print illustrations from your disk files.

5. The publisher may ask you to submit computer files of your illustrations. If so, find out how the files should be formatted and stored. Drawing programs often create large files that require huge disk space. They may have to be condensed to store on floppies before shipping.

6. Consult with your editor before you have the costly glossy prints or micrographs prepared. Sometimes, illustrations may have to be photographed to produce glossy prints that are submitted with the final version of the manuscript. Also, some illustrations may be photomicrographs prepared on a special equipment. When submitting photomicrographs, specify the degree of magnification.

7. Have a professional photographer take pictures of illustrations (other than photographs) that you wish to borrow from another publication. The professional will take a picture with a graphics camera to produce high quality black and white matte prints.

8. Submit a few representative samples of finished line art to the in-house editor who will check them. Do this in the initial stage of writing. This will give you time to redesign or make changes in the artwork. Later revisions to artwork are costly and can delay publication of a text. To avoid this, prepare illustrations as soon as possible.

9. Include the original artwork with the initial manuscript submission Also submit a set of photocopies of your artwork.

10. Enclose the artwork in thick, stiff envelopes with pieces of cardboard inserted to prevent bending. Place tissue paper between figures to prevent them from rubbing and disfiguring each other. Place all figures for each chapter together and put them at the end of the chapter. Do not use staples or paper clips to hold them together. Do not attach the artwork to anything.

Color Figures

Reproduction of color art is extremely expensive. Avoid using color unless it is absolutely necessary. Discuss the need for color illustrations with your sponsoring editor before having them prepared. Also note that, although color figures can be converted to black and white prints, such conversions result in figures of poor quality. Therefore, it is better to print the figures originally in black and white.

Figure Captions and Legends

A **caption** is a description of a figure. A **legend** explains the symbols used in it. Each figure should have a brief caption. A figure caption should:

1. describe the figure sufficiently so that it can be understood without the text;
2. define all symbols and abbreviations used in the figure; and
3. give full credit to all borrowed illustrations.

Captions are not a part of the art work. They are typeset, not photographed. Therefore, type captions for each chapter **double-spaced on a separate sheet of paper** as the example shows:

Figure Caption

Figure 4-6. The vowel chart. Classification of English vowels based on the tongue position.

Note that each page on which a caption is placed has a heading ("Figure Caption"). The word "Figure" and its number are boldfaced. The caption is typed without indenting the first word.

Additional information needed to clarify the illustration may be placed in parentheses after the caption. Place figure captions at the end of each chapter.

If the Figure is borrowed from another source, obtain permission and give credit as the example shows:

> **Figure 4-6.** The vowel chart. Classification of English vowels based on the tongue position. *Note:* From *Phonetics*, by H. A. Higgins and C. L. Pickering, 1981, p. 37. New York: Pygmalion Publishing Company. Copyright 1981 by Pygmalion Publishing Company. Reprinted (or Adapted) by permission.

A **figure legend** is a part of the figure. Therefore, do not type the legend as it is not typeset. For example, the various symbols on an audiogram for the right and left ear thresholds are explained in the legend and are a part of the art work. When a figure is submitted as a glossy print, the legend (but not the caption) must be on it.

Figure Numbering and Citation in the Text

Number all figures consecutively with arabic numerals identifying both the chapter number and the figure number (e.g., Figure 4-6). Unless there is room to write the figure number at the very bottom of the page of line art, write the necessary information on the back as described under the section on photographs. Always use pencil to number art work.

In the text, you may refer to figures in various ways as shown, but the figure number is always specified:

> Hearing is tested in a specially constructed booth (see Figure 2-5).
> As shown in Figure 9-3, the hyoid bone . . .
> The temporal lobe is illustrated in Figure 10-5.

Do not write "the Figure 10-15 above/below" or "Figure on page 15" because the placement of figures on the typeset pages will not necessarily correspond to such references. A figure is always placed *after* it is cited in the text. Therefore, cite a figure as early in the section as is relevant. Citing or calling out a figure at the end of a relevant section may result in the figure being placed in the next (and irrelevant) section of the text. Calling out several figures simultaneously may lead to several consecutive pages of figures before the text resumes and disjointed figures and text discussions.

■ PERMISSIONS

Obtain permission to reproduce lengthy quotations, figures, tables, and other material from another published or unpublished source from all who hold the copyright. You must receive permission from both the authors and publishers. Also, get a signed consent from all persons in photographs you wish to use. When you photograph children, get permission from their parents or legal guardians. In addition, have the professional photographers who take the pictures sign a form to release the rights to their pictures (see Appendix B).

Your in-house editor can answer your questions about permissions, but the following list should help you determine what materials require permission:

1. Tables, charts, figures, photographs, and other illustrations taken from another copyrighted source
2. Prose passage of 250 words or more
3. Scattered passages from a single work that cumulatively amount to 250 words or more
4. A passage less than 250 words that constitutes more than 5% of a work or is a complete use in itself (e.g., a very brief chapter)
5. All quotations from copyrighted music, lyrics to songs, or poetry
6. Extracts of any length from unpublished sources, such as theses, dissertations, lecture notes, and letters (these are protected by common-law copyright and require permission of the author)
7. Cartoons or similar material
8. Quotations from newspapers and magazines
9. Illustrations, graphs, or other kinds of artwork taken from a copyrighted computer software program

Permission is *not* needed if the material in your book is based on, or extensively revised from, the original. Materials that have been adapted to a significant extent and those that are in public domain do not require permission. A work is in the public domain if it (1) was published in the United States without valid copyright, (2) the copyright has expired, or (3) it is taken from a U.S. government publication, provided the material has not appeared previously in copyrighted form. But **in all such cases, credit the original source**. If you are not sure about the status of the copyright of material you wish to reproduce, contact the Library of Congress to check copyright expiration dates.

Publishers and authors may require a fee to be paid for the permission to reproduce their material. The author must obtain these permissions and pay the fees. Therefore, before including materials from other sources, contact the copyright holder to make sure that the permission is readily available and the fees are affordable. Getting permission from some sources, especially from the estate of a trade book author, can take several months and require repeated contacts. Delayed permission for a single illustration can hold up the production of a book.

Many illustrations, including photographs of industrial or commercial products, may be obtained from various manufacturers. For example, manufacturers of hearing aids, audiometers, and various laboratory instruments readily provide authors with pictures and permission to reproduce them. Whenever possible, obtain pictures from manufacturers. These pictures are professionally prepared for print publicity and are given free of charge. Please do obtain written permission to use them in your text.

Acknowledgment for illustrations reproduced from other sources is typed at the end of the figure caption as shown in the two examples:

Example 1

Figure 6-8. The neuron. *Note*: From *Anatomy and physiology* (p. 29) by B. S. Brain and H. S. Hand, 1991, Graveville, OH: Skeleton Publishing Company. Copyright 1991 by the Skeleton Publishing Company. Reprinted by permission.

Example 2

Figure 10-2. A computerized speech signal processor. (Photo courtesy of Chatterbox Corporation.)

Reprints

Lengthy selections of copyrighted material, such as a complete chapter or a section of a chapter to be reprinted in a text, should be submitted as tear sheets. Mount each original page on an 8½ × 11 inch sheet of paper with rubber cement or masking tape.

A tear sheet is the actual page cut from the book or journal. You need two copies of the source to prepare a complete set of tear sheets when the selection has been printed on both sides of paper. Along with the tear sheets of the text, submit the tear sheets of the title page and copyright page of the book or journal. If you cannot submit tear sheets, submit fine quality photocopies made from the original mounted according to the previous instructions.

If you plan to edit the material before it is reprinted, inform the copyright holder and send a copy of the edited form when you request permission. You must get permission to edit *and* reproduce the material.

In your editing, make sure that all the wording made incorrect by the new context (e.g., "In the last chapter . . ." or references to figure numbers in the original publication) has been deleted or amended.

Permission Forms

Your publisher has various kinds of permission forms. Obtain them from your in-house editor. Samples of a few commonly used permission forms are included in Appendix B. You may photocopy them for your use.

Carefully examine the permission forms you receive from copyright holders. The form specifies the scope of the permission granted by copyright holders. Some copyright holders limit the use of their material to the first edition of your book; others limit it to a certain number of copies. Still other publishers limit the use to books distributed only in the United States. Some publishers also specify wording of the credit line to be used. Check each permission granted and make changes as needed in permission lines. It is important to take note of these limitations because they will determine whether or not you seek permission again for the second edition, for a foreign publication, or for foreign distribution of your book published in the United States.

■ REFERENCES

Cite only a few essential references in undergraduate texts. A carefully selected list of recommended readings may be more useful than an extended reference list. A reference list primarily documents and supports what is stated in a book or a research article. Many referenced articles are research papers published in journals. Sources not cited in the text are not referenced. To the contrary, recommended readings are other books or articles on the topic under discussion. These additional sources do not necessarily provide evidence supporting or justifying the statements made in the text. Instead, articles and books on a reading list supplement the text. They may provide more details or approach the subject matter from a different perspective. Some books on the recommended reading list may be literary works of interest. Many of these works may not have been cited in the text.

Please pay careful attention to the selection of references, citation of references in the text, and to the preparation of the reference list. Much editorial time can be saved if the text citations are identical to the reference list. A reference checklist is provided in Appendix D.

Use the Fourth Edition of the *Publication Manual of the American Psychological Association* (1994) as a guide to citing references in the text. Prepare the reference list according to the *Manual* except for indentation of the first line of each reference entry. Do not indent the first line and prepare the reference list as described later in this manual.

When you are the sole author of the book, consider whether to have a reference list for every chapter or one for the entire book. A preferred strategy is to list the recommended readings at the end of each chapter and to have a single reference list at the end of book. When each chapter has a reference list, some repetition is unavoidable. A single reference list for the book is economical and time saving. In any case, discuss this with your editor before making a final decision.

Each chapter in an edited book with multiple authors should have its own reference list. A single reference list in edited books makes it difficult to retrieve the sources and to ensure accuracy.

Reference Citation in Chapters of a Text

In citing **one work by a single author in the text**, cite the author's last name and the year of publication. When the author's name is part of the narrative, only the year of publication is placed in parentheses:

> In his study of heavy weight champions, Byson (1989) found that . . .

> Byson (1989) found that the reaction time of boxers . . .

Omit the year when the same study is referred to again within the same paragraph if it cannot be confused with another study:

> Byson (1989) found that the reaction time of his opponents was sluggish . . . Byson also found that . . .

When neither the name nor the year is a part of the narrative, enclose both within parentheses:

> A study showed that boxing causes brain damage (Hali, 1990).

Occasionally, the year also may be a part of narration; if so, do not enclose it in parentheses:

> In 1978, MacVinro was the first to suggest that playing tennis can build ego strength.

Always cite both the names when a work has **two authors**:

> Tang and Lagassi (1990) discovered that college courses are incomprehensible.

A study found that courses on basket weaving are not a piece of cake (Hali & Byson, 1990).

Cite works with **three to five authors** using all the authors' names the first time. Subsequently, cite only the first author's last name and add "et al." to it; also include the year of publication:

In a study on head injury, Hali, Byson, and Tedson (1972) found that . . . (first citation)

The results of Hali et al. (1972) were that . . . (subsequent citation)

In their study on vocal nodules, Lordon, Fontana, Tanseko, Tavratinova, and Pendl (1989) discovered that . . . (first citation)

Lordon et al. (1989) showed that . . . (subsequent citation)

Note that there is no period after "et" and "et al." is not underlined or italicized.

If two studies published in the same year with a different combination of multiple authors have the same first author, cite all names. For example, one study by Lordon, Fontana, Tanseko, and Pendl (1990) and another by Lordon, Hali, Byson, Tavratinova, and Fontana (1990) both shorten to Lordon et al. (1990). In such cases, cite all names.

Cite works of **six or more authors** by the last name of the first author only, even in the first citation. Add "et al." and the year in parentheses.

In citing two such studies of different combination of six or more authors published in the same year, add as many additional names as are needed to distinguish the two studies and end it with "et al." and the year of publication in parentheses:

Bang, Fang, and Wang et al. (1990) have reported that . . . (This study was done by seven authors: Bang, Fang, Wang, Song, Long, Mong, and Tong)

Bang, Fang, Wang, and Song et al. (1990) have shown that . . . (This study was done by six authors: Bang, Fang, Wang, Song, Zong, and Gong)

Join **multiple names** with *and* when the citation is part of the narrative; when the citation is in parentheses, join the names with an ampersand (&):

Hecker and Donnors (1985) showed that . . .

The frequency of spitting on the field is related to the number of hits (Rosen & Tonseko, 1988).

Cite **multiple authors with the same last name** with their initials every time they are cited:

Z. X. Connors (1986) and Q. X. Connors (1968) reported that . . .

As discussed by Z. X. Connors et al. (1986) and Q. X. Connors (1968) . . .

Cite **multiple works by the same author** as follows:

Studies show that the more exciting the game, the greater the injury to vocal cords (Fontana, 1985, 1987, 1990, in press).

Data suggest that yells that induce vocal nodules are exciting (Rosery & Ruthery, 1975, 1978, 1981).

Attach suffixes a, b, c, and so on to the year when citing **multiple works by the same author, published in the same year**:

Several studies (Johnson, 1975a, 1975b, 1975c, in press-a, in press-b)

Studies have shown that ball game watching increases brain size (Tonseko, 1985a, 1985b, 1985c; Fontana, 1988a, 1988b, in press-a, in press-b).

Note that the year is repeated; do not write 1988a, b, c. The assignment of a, b, c, and so on to studies published in the same year is done by alphabetizing the first word of title of articles. Also, names are separated by semicolons.

Arrange the last names of **multiple authors** within parentheses in alphabetical order, separating each name with a semicolon:

(Began, 1980; Lord, 1975; Push, 1989; Zoom, 1990).

(Began & Quinn, 1980; Lord, Horde, & Board, 1975; Push & Twink, 1991)

Note that when a work has *multiple authors*, the last name of the first author determines the order in which the names are typed. The names are separated by semicolons; there is no *and* or & before the last citation; an ampersand joins the names of two authors of the same work typed within parentheses.

Reference List

A reference list includes only sources that are cited in the text. A bibliography includes all, or all noteworthy, publications on a given topic or line of investigation. Textbooks **do not have bibliographies**; only the sources cited in the text are listed as references.

Some computer word-processing programs can print all the text citations at the end of a chapter. If this is possible, you have at least all the names listed. Additional information, including the title of the book or the journal and the name of the publisher must be added to the list.

Prepare the reference list according to the APA *Manual* (4th ed., 1994). The suggestions offered here are based on the *Manual*; however, the format recommended here has some notable exceptions.

Start the reference list on a new page with a centered, all capitalized heading:

REFERENCES

Type all entries in the reference list **double spaced**. Single-spaced reference lists are difficult to edit.

Type the first line of each entry flush left and the subsequent lines indented three spaces. On most word processors, this is accomplished by setting the **hanging indent** at three character spaces. *Note that this is different from the format for reference lists specified in the fourth edition of APA Manual (1994), which requires the first line to be indented and the subsequent lines to be typed flush left.* Because this regular paragraph format makes it difficult to pick names from the reference list, it is recommended that you retain the format of the third edition for reference lists. See examples given in the next section.

Arrange the reference list alphabetically. Double check to make sure that:

1. All sources cited in the text are accurately listed in the reference list; and, the names of authors are spelled identically in the text citation and reference list.
2. Sources not cited in the text are not included in the reference list.

Recall that you may place sources not cited in the text on the short list of **recommended readings**, although even these are likely to be cited in the text.

When revising the manuscript, you may delete a portion of the text and some references with it. If so, immediately remove the citations in the reference list as well. Deleting or adding references after the manuscript is typeset is expensive and the cost may be charged to the author.

Abbreviations Used in Reference Lists

Use the following abbreviations in the reference list (APA *Manual*, 1994):

chap.	Chapter
ed.	edition
rev. ed.	revised edition
2nd ed.	second edition
Ed. (Eds.)	Editor (Editors)
Trans.	Translator(s)
p. (pp.)	page (pages)
Vol.	Volume (as in Vol. 7)
vols.	volumes (as in 9 vols.)
No.	Number
Pt.	Part
Tech. Rep.	Technical Report
Suppl.	Supplement

All names of states and territories of the United States are abbreviated according to the two-letter U.S. Postal Service abbreviations:

Alabama	AL	Kentucky	KY
Alaska	AK	Louisiana	LA
American Samoa	AS	Maine	ME
Arizona	AZ	Maryland	MD
Arkansas	AR	Massachusetts	MA
California	CA	Michigan	MI
Canal Zone	CZ	Minnesota	MN
Colorado	CO	Mississippi	MS
Connecticut	CT	Missouri	MO
Delaware	DE	Montana	MT
District of Columbia	DC	Nebraska	NE
Florida	FL	Nevada	NV
Georgia	GA	New Hampshire	NH
Guam	GU	New Jersey	NJ
Hawaii	HI	New Mexico	NM
Idaho	ID	New York	NY
Illinois	IL	North Carolina	NC
Indiana	IN	North Dakota	ND
Iowa	IA	Ohio	OH
Kansas	KS	Oklahoma	OK

Oregon	OR	Utah	UT
Pennsylvania	PA	Vermont	VT
Puerto Rico	PR	Virginia	VA
Rhode Island	RI	Virgin Islands	VI
South Carolina	SC	Washington	WA
South Dakota	SD	West Virginia	WV
Tennessee	TN	Wisconsin	WI
Texas	TX	Wyoming	WY

Alphabetical Order in the Reference List

Arrange the reference list alphabetically. Follow these rules in preparing the list:

1. For works by multiple authors, the surname of the first author determines the placement in the list.
2. Names are alphabetized letter by letter, but the initials are excluded: Thomas, Z. X., precedes Thomson, A. B. According to the APA *Manual* (1994), this follows the rule "nothing precedes something."
3. Prefixes are also arranged in their strict alphabetical order. An apostrophe attached to a prefix (M') is not considered. *Mac* precedes *Mc* (MacMinnan before McNeil).
4. Consult the biographical section of Webster's *New Collegiate Dictionary* to find the order in which surnames with articles and prepositions are arranged (names with de, la, du, von, etc.).
5. Several works by the same author, but some with and some without co-authors, are listed starting with those works that do not have co-authors:

   Tonseko, K. J. (1985).
   Tonseko, K. J. (1988).
   Tonseko, K. J., & Fontana, P. J. (1982).
   Tonseko, K. J., & Lordon, T. P. (1984).

   Note that several works by the same single author are arranged according to the year of publication, starting with the earliest year. Second and subsequent authors' names are also alphabetized.

6. In arranging titles of several works published by the same author in the same year, alphabetize them according to the titles. Such words as *A* and *The* at the beginning of the title are ignored. The lowercase letters a, b, c, and so on are attached to the year of publication:

Lagassi, A. R. (1991a). Advantages of short-handled rackets.
Lagassi, A. R. (1991b). Problems of clay courts.

7. In listing different authors of the same last name, alphabetize according to the initials:

Tavratinova, B. D. (1987).
Tavratinova, S. N. (1986).

8. In listing works with corporate, agency, or institutions as authors, alphabetize the name with the first significant word. Spell out the full name:

American Psychological Association (not APA)
American Speech-Language-Hearing Association (not ASHA)
National Institute on Deafness and other Communication Disorders (not NIDCD).

Updating References

As you revise your manuscript, update your references. By the time you prepare the final version of your manuscript, some of the books you cited originally may have been revised. Articles you initially cited as "in press" may have been published. Therefore, before you submit the final version of your manuscript, update your citations and references (see Appendix D).

■ SELECTED EXAMPLES OF REFERENCES

The APA *Manual* (1994) contains many examples of references. In this section, sample references that are most likely to be included in a textbook are given. The reader must consult the APA *Manual* for a more thorough list of samples.

Journal Articles

Bultit, B. S., Airhead, E. H., & Longwind, H. A. (1990). Intervening variables in human behavior: Thirty years of theorizing. *Journal of Theories Unlimited, 98*, 38–178.

Hazlenut, L. M., & Beachnut P. M. (in press). Nutty theories in naughty disciplines. *Journal of Speculative Psychology.*

Lordon, M. S., & Bellwae, T. M. (1987). The offensive tactics on the football field and delayed aphasic symptoms. *Journal of Speech and Hearing Disorders, 42*, 50–58.

McVenro, J. P. (1990). The relation between umpire judgments and player verbal outbursts. *Journal of Verbal Abuse, 50,* 230-240.

Platos, I., & Tottle, A. (1996). The effects of an instructor's mental wanderings on student learning in the classroom. *Journal of Modern Education, 55*(3), 90-150.

Note that in typing a journal article in the reference list:

1. After the last initial, a space is given. After the year in parentheses, a period is typed and **one** space is given before starting the article title.
2. The names of two authors are joined by an ampersand (&) and the first author's initials are followed by a comma.
3. Only the first letter of the article title or subtitle is capitalized. **One** space is given before the journal name is typed.
4. All important words of the journal name are capitalized; journal titles are not abbreviated; and the entire title is italicized or underlined. The APA *Manual* (1994) requires underlining only, but in text preparation, italicizing is fine.
5. The volume number is italicized (or underlined as per APA *Manual,* 1994); the word *volume* or its abbreviation is not used.
6. The issue number of a journal, typed only when the pages of individual issues of a given volume are numbered separately (not consecutively), is placed within parentheses immediately following the volume number. The issue number is *not* underlined or italicized, and there is *no space* between the volume number and the opening parenthesis.
7. The last entry is the page number or numbers without *p.* or *pp.*
8. For an article in press, the date, volume number, and page number are not given. The year of publication is replaced by the words "in press." (Update the status of articles listed as "in press" during each stage of manuscript preparation.)
9. The reference list is prepared with a hanging indent of three spaces. The first line of each reference is **not** indented and the second and subsequent lines are indented **three spaces** (both contrary to the APA *Manual,* 1994 requirement).

Books

American Psychological Association. (1994). *Publication Manual of the American Psychological Association* (4th ed.). Washington, DC: Author.

Boczquats, N. S. (1990). *Oceanography and communication: A new frontier.* Chicago: Blue Haven Press.

Histrionik, K. L., Jr., & Stoic, P. L. (1975). *Neurotic behavior* (2nd ed.). Los Angeles: Angeles Publishing Company.

Kosquitenski, P. S., & Pattent, T. P. (1984). *Communicative disorders in the bees.* New York: Bacmillan.

Null, B. D. (1988). *Numbers in civilization* (rev. ed.). New York: Sappleton.

Note that in referencing books:

1. The title of the book is italicized or underlined. Only the first letter of the title and subtitle are capitalized.
2. One space is used between the year and the title and between the title and the place of publication.
3. The abbreviated word *Jr.*, is typed after the last initial.
4. The edition number or the words "rev. ed." (for revised edition) are typed after the title, without a period, and placed within parentheses as shown.
5. The publishing company's name is typed exactly as it appears in the book being referenced.
6. In case of books written and published by corporations, agencies, or associations, the word "Author" is typed for the publisher.

Edited Books and Chapters in Edited Books

Baker, K. V. (1990). The unknown and the unconscious. In C. Hart (Ed.), *Unknown states of consciousness* (pp. 305-395). New York: Mystery Publishing House.

Henn, N. S. (1994). The mind of chickens. In S. N. Quinn & N. S. Chinn (Eds.). *Mind matters* (2nd ed., pp. 5-505).

Hunt, C. P., & Holms, G. S. (Eds.). (1995). *Mysteries of mental events.* San Francisco: Invisible Publishers.

Mann, P. T. (Ed.). (1996). *The innate language.* (Vols. 1-50). Los Angeles: The Primate Press.

Onus, B. (1995). Mental connections and moral responsibility. In T. T. Dement & D. D. Right (Eds.), *Handbook of morality: Vol. 25. Mind and morality* (pp. 2050-2195). Boston: Righteous Press.

Quest, K. O. (1993). Thirst as a form of cognitive urge to seek knowledge. In Z. Hung (Ed.), *Sensation and knowledge seeking* (Vol. 99, pp. 3-59). Chicago: Sensation Press.

Note that in referencing edited books or chapters in edited books:

1. The abbreviated word (Ed.) for one editor or (Eds.) for multiple editors is typed in parentheses.
2. While (ed.) refers to an edition of a book, (Ed.) refers to an editor.
3. The editor's initials should be at the beginning, not the end of the surname.
4. When a chapter is cited from an edited book, the page numbers of the chapter must be typed after the title and placed within parentheses.
5. The edition or volume number of an edited book should be typed, within parentheses, after the title of the edited book and before the page numbers (Vol. 99, pp. 3-59; or, 2nd ed., pp. 22-34).
6. The specific title of a volume in a series should be typed after the title of the series and the volume number (*Handbook of morality: Vol. 25. Mind and morality* (pp. 2050-2195).

Reports from Organizations and Government Agencies

National Child Health and Human Development. (1910). *How not to write research proposals.* (DHHS Publication No. QRS-00910). Washington, DC: U.S. Government Printing Office.

Norm, J. J. (1989). *Invariably fixed stages of cognitive development.* (Report No. 15). Washington, DC: National Cognition Association.

Proceedings of Conferences and Conventions

Peacok, P. L., & Lyon, A. D. (1990). Cooperation within the animal kingdom. In E. L. Phant & H. I. Pottoms (Eds.), *Proceedings of the Ninety Fourth International Symposium on the Animal Kingdom* (pp. 23-57). Boston: Cobra Press.

Convention Presentations

Idlemann, P. S. (1983, November). *Variables related to doing nothing.* Paper presented at the Annual Convention of the American Anti-workaholic Association, Bullhead City, AZ.

Note that the title of an unpublished paper presented at a convention is italicized (or underlined) and that the month and location of the meeting are included in the reference.

Unpublished Articles, Theses, or Dissertations

Dimm, B. J. (1975). *Why some articles do not get published.* Unpublished manuscript.

Brightly, B. B. (1975). *The complex relationship between self image, hair color, and academic learning in children from low, medium, and high income levels.* Unpublished master's thesis, Sharp College of Education, Needles, CA.

Smiley, S. S. (1985). *Variables related to early or late toilet training and the frequency of smiling in high school classrooms.* Unpublished doctoral dissertation, Haywire University, Lynn, OH.

Note that the titles of unpublished articles, theses, and dissertations are italicized (or underlined).

■ BACK MATTER

Appendixes

Keep the number of appendixes to a minimum in textbooks. Use appendixes to provide related and useful information that cannot be integrated into the text. In textbooks, inclusion of published materials such as tests, entire chapters from other books, and so forth is not recommended. Also, do not write extensive notes related to specific chapters which the students are expected to read; most students do not read them. Give all essential information in the text.

Start each appendix on a new page with a centered heading (Appendix) typed at the top of the page. Add letters A, B, and so forth if you have multiple appendixes. If you have only one appendix, do not add A to it. Using the uppercase and lowercase letters, type the title of the appendix double-spaced, centered and underlined; begin the text of the appendix after four spaces (two returns on the keyboard when the paragraph is formatted double spaced); double space all lines:

Appendix

Journals Published by the American Speech-Language-Hearing Association

Appendix A

Abbreviations Used in Medicine

Indexes

A subject index is essential for textbooks. An author index may be useful or required by certain publishers. Consult your editor about author indexes.

A carefully prepared subject index will help students find information on specific topics quickly and easily. All defined terms, technical concepts, procedures, theories, and other important bits of information must be indexed. Some amount of cross-indexing is essential. In cross-indexing, the same terms or concepts may appear under different headings (e.g., "assessment" and "differential diagnosis"; "speech disorders," and then a separate entry for such specific disorders as "stuttering," and "voice disorders").

An author index, although less crucial, may be required for the sake of accuracy and scholarly documentation of information. The author index is arranged in the alphabetical order of authors' last names. An author's last name, initials, and the page number(s) on which the author is cited in the text are given in the index.

Before you prepare an index, study indexes in a few books similar to yours to get an idea of their organization. You also can consult one of the books on indexing included in this *Manual's* bibliography.

There are software programs that generate indexes. Your word processor may offer some assistance in preparing indexes. Important terms and concepts printed in bold script are easily spotted for indexing. The names on the reference list may be copied into the author index document. The search function may be used to locate certain terms in the document. Some word processors search names and print them alphabetically. But mostly, you must generate the entries of your subject index.

Usefulness is the single most important criterion of subject index entries. Each entry, when looked up in the text, should give some meaningful information to the reader.

Do not index the following:

1. Terms and names mentioned only in the preface, dedication, and acknowledgment.
2. Terms that are mentioned incidentally for which there is no substantial information when looked up.
3. Terms that the typical reader will not look up in that book. For instance, if you mentioned a geological fault in a book on stuttering, do not index the fault.
4. Chapter headings and subheadings.
5. Tables and illustrations.

Preparation of subject indexes takes time. Therefore, prepare the basic entries when the completed manuscript goes to the reviewers. Add the page numbers when you receive the page proofs.

If you wish, the publisher will hire a professional indexer to prepare your indexes. You will be given an estimate of the cost that will be charged against the royalties. When you are ready to prepare your indexes, contact one of the editors who may give additional information.

5 Manuscript Editing and Prepublication Reviews

Textbook writing, even when a single author is involved, is a team effort. Preparation of textbooks is facilitated by a team of editors and consultants who work with the author to ensure currency and accuracy of information presented. Editors and editorial consultants (readers) also help ensure appropriateness and suitability of coverage and writing style for the intended level of instruction. The first editor you will come in contact with is most likely an acquisitions editor or an in-house editor of the publishing house. In other cases, you may come in contact with a textbook series editor.

Publishing houses do everything possible to help authors complete their manuscripts in a timely manner. Good publishing houses invest in editors who can provide competent and timely advise and help to authors. In considering a publishing house, authors should find out, among such other things as marketing ability, the amount and quality of editorial help it offers its authors. Once you sign a book contract with a publisher, the editors who work with you are on your side. Their job is to offer you the needed assistance, guidance, and feedback on your work so that the project is brought to fruition.

■ THE IN-HOUSE EDITOR

An in-house editor is an editor employed by a publishing house. An in-house editor also may be an acquisitions editor. Acquisition editors contact potential authors of textbooks to acquire new manuscripts for the publishing house. When authors contact a publishing house with a book proposal or a completed manuscript, they are likely to communicate with an acquisitions editor.

The in-house editor is responsible for all aspects of manuscript preparation until it is sent to the production department. The in-house editor reviews each manuscript to make sure that it conforms to the agreed-upon organization and content. When there is no textbook series editor, the in-house editor recruits consulting editors, sends the manuscript for expert review, and channels the reviews with his or her own comments to the author.

You should maintain a constant contact with the in-house editor who is knowledgeable about many aspects of publication. The in-house editor typically is not responsible for producing and marketing your book. Nonetheless, the editor will refer you to appropriate persons within the company if you have questions about production and publication of your book. All contractual matters concerning your book may be discussed with the in-house editor. Your in-house editor is your main contact person with the publishing company.

■ THE SERIES EDITOR

As noted in Chapter 1, there often is a series editor who, with the in-house editor, works on a series of books on a specific topic, area of investigation, or several texts on different subjects. The series editor is an expert in the discipline who has significant experience in writing and editing. Most series editors work as consultants to publishing houses. They often work at various universities and thus are not employees of publishing houses. In many cases, you will work simultaneously with an in-house editor and a series editor. When you sign a contract to write a text, find out who does what to help you complete your book.

The series editor reviews each manuscript in the series. The series editor's job is to evaluate the manuscript for its content, style, organization, accuracy, and appropriateness. In all stages of writing, you may receive specific feedback from the series editor. It is helpful for you to send the first chapter to the series editor and discuss the general writing strategy, scope, content, and appropriateness for the intended level of instruction. Systematic and extensive feedback on the first chapter will help avoid excessive revisions of subsequent chapters. Therefore, your series editor is a main resource person whose job it is to help shape the organization and content of the book. The editor will do everything possible to help you complete the book in a timely and efficient manner.

The series editor will select expert reviewers of your manuscript. Depending on the nature of the book, one or more experts may review your manuscript. Such reviews are usually anonymous and are sent directly to the editor. The editor then sends the reviews to the author along with his or her comments and suggestions.

■ CONSULTING EXPERT'S REVIEW

Consulting experts are selected for their ability to make thorough reviews of manuscripts to provide constructive feedback to authors. The role of the reviewers is to evaluate the manuscript to assure accuracy, currency, and adequacy of information covered by the author. The reviewer also will be asked to judge the appropriateness of both the content and the writing level for the intended audience. The series editor may pose specific questions to the reviewers and seek their advice about the manuscript.

The series and the in-house editors may provide feedback to you before the manuscript is sent to the reviewers. In such cases, you will have a chance to revise the manuscript before it is submitted to outside reviewers. In other cases, the two editors may wait until they receive the reviews to give feedback. If you have a preference in this matter, contact your series editor.

Some editors and expert consultants concentrate on content of the manuscript and appropriate presentation for the level of intended instruction and leave editing for mechanics to the copy editor. Other editors give extensive feedback on mechanics as well, although generally the copy editor will still find much to do to improve a manuscript.

■ PROMPT AND CAREFUL REVISIONS

You are urged to revise the manuscript promptly and carefully as soon as you receive feedback from different editors and reviewers at different stages of writing. Author procrastination in revising manuscripts is a major cause of costly and unnecessary delays in book publication, especially after the book has been "launched" by the publishing house. Note that once the book has been launched, the publisher begins coordinated marketing efforts on behalf of your book. Publication delay then may cause reduced or canceled sales if the book is not available as scheduled. Delays are costly to both you and the publisher.

In revising the manuscript, pay special attention to questions raised about the validity of information. Factual errors sometime creep into text writing, especially when a single author writes on a wide range of topics. Therefore, take seriously even a hint of a factual error and double check your writing and its sources.

Although critics may be sometimes wrong, they are usually right when they point out unclear writing. If scholarly readers did not understand something you wrote, most students will not either. Critics also often are correct when they argue that a chapter or a section is too long and that the material can be written adequately in fewer pages. To reduce length, you need not always eliminate material. Say all you must, but in fewer words. Reduce redundancy and wordiness.

Consider each suggestion seriously, even when your initial reaction is to reject some of them. Sometimes, you may feel like rejecting a suggestion because of its unpleasant tone and abruptness. Occasionally, the merit of a suggestion may be masked by a reviewer's imperious disposition. But on further reflection, most suggestions, including those offered without tact, tend to appear reasonable and acceptable. Take all suggestions, especially those that are highly critical of your writing, as opportunities to improve the text. If certain suggestions are still not acceptable, justify your writing. Editors respect your considered judgment because you are the expert who wrote the book.

■ FINAL SUBMISSION OF THE MANUSCRIPT

The manuscript you revise according to the comments you receive from the in-house editor, the series editor, and consulting experts results in a final version of the manuscript that is submitted to the in-house editor. This version is final only in the sense that most of the content and organization of the book is completed. Essentially, the manuscript is acceptable to experts in the subject matter; it has been edited and revised mostly for content, coverage, and organization. The manuscript will be edited one more time before it is typeset. This editing is done by a copy editor. Copyediting is done mostly for mechanics of writing, but some content-related editing to improve clarity and consistency of presentation also are part of it. Following this editing, the manuscript will be revised one more time. Copyediting, however, is normally a part of the book production process. Therefore, copyediting and the author's subsequent final revision are described in the next chapter.

Send the original of the revised manuscript to the in-house editor along with the computer disks and original artwork. Enclose a printed copy of all the art work. Send a copy of the manuscript to the series editor.

6 Production of Textbooks

The in-house editor who receives the final version of the manuscript reviews it one more time to make sure that various comments offered to the author were considered and necessary changes were made. The editor will review your justification for rejecting editorial suggestions. The in-house editor also may receive a final feedback from the textbook series editor. This feedback may often be verbal in which the series editor approves the final version of the manuscript sent to the publishing house.

The in-house editor's main concern at this point is the completeness of the manuscript submitted. The editor will check the artwork or other forms of illustrations and the front and the back matter. If everything is satisfactory, the in-house editor will initiate the launch meeting.

■ THE LAUNCH MEETING

A meeting of the in-house editor and staff of both the marketing and production departments is conducted to "launch" your book. A launch meeting is the beginning of the book production process. In this meeting, a definite timeline for publication of your book is set. The size and design of your book are discussed, and a tentative marketing plan is designed.

Following this meeting, the marketing department will contact you to discuss your ideas or suggestions for marketing the book. The production department will contact you to discuss the cover, book design, and production schedule for your book. The staff in the production department will be in touch with you until the book is printed, bound, and published.

■ THE PRODUCTION MANAGER/EDITOR

Once your book is launched, it will move from the in-house editor to the production manager (or editor) who sets up a production schedule and shepherds your book from this point to the printer. Your book will pass through several hands to be copyedited, typeset, proofread, and indexed before it is sent to the printer. Your primary contact throughout this process is the production manager.

Unlike the editorial process, the production process moves very quickly. Because the production process does not allow for undue delays, you should be prepared to respond quickly throughout the various stages of book production. The following are the general book production guidelines and timelines. Contact your production manager for specific guidelines and variations.

■ THE COPY EDITOR'S FEEDBACK

The production manager sends the manuscript to a copy editor who is an expert in copyediting manuscripts. The copy editor's main concerns are stylistic matters along with consistency and clarity. The copy editor edits the manuscript for spelling, punctuation, capitalization, grammatical problems, and many other stylistic matters. He or she also will edit to clear any remaining sentence structure problems, suggest ways of simplifying sentences, and offer other suggestions to further improve the readability of the manuscript. The copy editor also checks the consistency with which the author has used different levels of heading and suggests needed changes. Furthermore, the copy editor checks the accuracy of references and agreement between reference citations within the text and the reference list. The copy editor ensures that the book is consistent with the style the publishing house uses (e.g., specific styles recommended by the American Psychological Association, the *Chicago Manual of Style,* or the American Medical Association).

The copy editor usually is not an expert in the subject matter. Therefore, generally, the copy editor does not offer substantive comments on the content of the book. However, some content-related editing is unavoidable in case of unclear writing and vague explanations or descriptions. For the most part, though, the copy editor reads the manuscript as an educated outsider with expertise in stylistic matters. The comments offered by the copy editor are valuable in giving the manuscript its final, polished look.

When the copy editor is finished, generally 2 weeks from the launch meeting, the production manager will send you the manuscript for final revision. In most cases, you will have a week to 10 days to revise the manuscript and answer the copy editor's questions.

The copy editor's suggestions usually are made on the manuscript itself. Copy editors use proofreading symbols to make changes on the manuscript, some of which may not be familiar to you. Please consult Appendix E, which contains a chart of the most commonly used proofreading symbols. If you do not understand some of the changes made by the copy editor or are not clear which changes you should make, call the production manager for clarification.

The copyedited manuscript also includes abbreviations written in the margins. These abbreviations specify design elements intended for the typesetter and not the author. Generally, these codes are made in different color ink than the copyediting done on the manuscript.

The copy editor's suggested substantive changes will be accompanied by a query. The copy editor also will query you about missing or inconsistent information. You should answer these queries, either by making the appropriate changes in the manuscript copy or by a note on the manuscript margin.

Occasionally, a copy editor's suggested revision of sentences may be mistaken or misleading or may cause misinterpretation of technical information. In such cases, you may reinstate the original sentence. Better yet, rewrite the sentence because the revision was probably suggested for a good reason.

Please note that this is your final opportunity to make extensive revisions to the manuscript. Changes made later, at the proof stage, are both time-consuming and expensive and all publishers strongly discourage them. Before sending it to the production manager, review the entire revised manuscript to ensure that you are satisfied with it.

After reviewing the copy editor's changes, enter all of the copyediting changes, along with any other changes you wish to make on the disks. Print out a revised copy of the manuscript. Send the new print-out along with the revised disks and the original copy-edited manuscript to the production manager. Before shipping, make sure you have kept the original disks and made a set of back-up disks containing the final, copy-edited version of your manuscript. Remember to label each disk you send with your name, an abbreviated version of the title of your book, the computer and word-processing program you used to prepare the manuscript, and the file names of the chapters included on each disk.

If you are sending artwork on disk, make sure that you have saved all art files appropriately (see Chapter 4) and include a list of file names. Print each figure at no less than 600 dpi and enclose printed copies with the disks and the manuscript.

Always send your manuscript and disks via next day air delivery service. This will ensure receipted and timely delivery.

When you return the manuscript, a production manager or editor will check your revisions for accuracy and to ensure that the copy editor's questions have all been answered. The production editor also will determine the interior design of the pages and mark the manuscript for the typesetter in the page design selected. The manuscript is then sent to a typesetter.

■ PROOFS AND PROOFREADING

The typesetter uses your disks to format book pages and place the art and tables in appropriate textual contexts. When this process is complete, generally in about 2 weeks, the production manager sends you a set of page proofs for your careful proofreading. Some publishers will first send you galley proofs and then page proofs. **Galley proofs** are continuous long sheets of papers on which the initial printing is done. No pages will have been formed, and figures and tables will not be integrated with the text. **Page proofs** correctly show all the formed pages, figures, tables, and all front and back matter arranged in their proper order. At the same time you are reading the proofs, a professional proofreader also will be reading the page proofs. If you are not indexing the text, an indexer will be preparing the index.

Read the proofs carefully and correct all typographic errors. Double check the headings, figures, tables, and their captions. Verify quotations, cross references to other chapters and page numbers, reference citations in the text, and the reference list. Make sure that the typesetter did not omit any part of the text and did not alter anything by mistake.

The single purpose of proofreading is to make sure that the **proofs agree with the copyedited manuscript**. This is not another opportunity to revise the manuscript. Therefore, avoid all temptations to rewrite when you proofread your page proofs. Correct only factual errors. For instance, the publication date of a book that has been revised since the submission of the copyedited manuscript should be updated. Such corrections (e.g., a change from 1993 to 1996) do not result in rearrangement of pages. All of these changes are author alterations. Typesetters will correct free of charge only the mistakes they made during typesetting. Any author alteration that shows a deviation from the manuscript submitted for typesetting, including the necessary corrections of factual errors, results in charges to the publisher who will then deduct them from the author's royalties.

Absolutely no addition or deletion of words is permitted at the page proof stage. A single phrase deleted or added may result in expensive re-arrangement of all subsequent pages in the text. Corrected page proofs must be sent back to the production department by express mail.

Proofreader's Marks

In correcting proofs, use proofreader's marks. The most commonly used marks are reproduced in Appendix E. Some dictionaries and most manuals of style contain a set of proofreader's marks. When you do not know a symbol or a mark for a correction, write the correction in the margin clearly and neatly. Suggest the place in the text where the correction must be inserted. Do not write corrections between the lines.

You will only be sending the corrected page proofs to the publisher, not your electronic manuscript. However, it is desirable to enter the changes you make on the page proofs into your electronic files of the manuscript. Otherwise, your version of the manuscript will not contain the final, printed version. This can create problems when you revise your book for subsequent editions.

You will have a week to 10 days to check the page proofs. It is very important to get to the proofs right away and complete the proofreading as quickly as possible. When you return the corrected page proofs, the production editor will incorporate your corrections with those of the proofreader, and send the pages back to the typesetter for final revisions. After making a final check to ensure that the typesetter has made all revisions, the production manager sends your book to the printer.

■ DESIGN OF A TEXT

Production managers welcome authors' suggestions regarding the lay-out of the book, the cover design, and other related matters. Talk to your production manager about your preferences as early as possible.

Offer your suggestions for a cover design, color of the cover, and typefaces to the staff of the production department. If you think of a design you like, make a rough sketch and send it to the staff. If you cannot make a sketch, talk to the staff about your ideas. An artist will work on your idea and send you a rough sketch of the book cover for your consideration. You can then discuss modifications in the design with the staff. If you like the design of certain published books, draw the production manager's attention to them.

■ AUTHOR'S HELP IN MARKETING THE BOOK

The marketing staff of the publishing house will prepare the publicity material to market your book. You may offer suggestions on how and to whom the book may be marketed. The marketing department will welcome your suggestions about new target audience to which the book may be promoted. You may write a short description of the book highlighting its strength, uniqueness, and intended audience and send it to the marketing staff.

As your book goes into production, contact the head of the marketing department to learn about the publishing house's plans for marketing your book. At that time, offer your suggestions. Help the marketing department produce the publicity material. Later, if you think of improvements in the printed and mailed publicity material, again contact the head of the marketing department with your suggestions.

7 Reprints and Revisions of Textbooks

You should maintain contact with your publisher after the book is published. Publishers send royalty statements once or twice a year, depending on your contract. You may want to keep track of sales figures. If there is a drop in sales, you should talk to the marketing staff to find out why. Maybe a new marketing strategy is needed. Or, the book may need a revised edition to better compete with newer books. The editorial and marketing staff at the publishing house may have found other reasons.

To maintain your textbook's currency, success, and usefulness to its consumers, you should maintain a close working relationship with your publisher. This means that you continue to work on reprints and revisions of your text.

■ REPRINTS OF TEXTBOOKS

Successful textbooks are reprinted several times before they are revised. A reprint is simply printing of additional copies of the same edition without substantive changes. As the stock on hand is depleted, the publisher will reprint textbooks. Although reprints do not allow for substantive changes in the content and format of books, they do provide opportunities to correct certain factual or typographic errors.

No matter how carefully you have checked your galleys and page proofs, some errors are likely to remain in the book. Most authors just wish to look at their book on the shelf with a justifiable sense of satisfaction. Having read many drafts of their book, they do not care to read it again. Still, it is necessary to carefully read the printed book and note any remaining factual or typographic errors. Make a list of these errors and their corrections. Add to this list the factual or typographic errors that instructors and students point out to you. Send the list of corrections to your production editor who keeps a correction file on each book. Because a book is reprinted whenever the publisher's stock is depleted, send your corrections soon after it is published. You can send additional corrections as and when you receive feedback from reviewers, colleagues, and students. Remind the production editor to make sure that the corrections are made in the next reprint.

■ REVISED EDITIONS OF TEXTBOOKS

A revised edition of a book, unlike a reprint, contains substantive changes. It may require new typesetting if you make significant changes throughout the text. In such cases, the revised edition will be copyedited as well.

Unlike monographs and books written for the general public, textbooks need to be revised periodically. There are several reasons for revising a textbook. Changes and advances in the discipline are the main reasons for revising a text. Newer texts compete with established texts by offering more recent information. Staying current is a main concern of all instructors, especially in scientific and professional disciplines. Writers of established texts then have to revise their texts to update information and thus compete well with newer texts.

There also is an economic reason for revising textbooks. Sales of even the most successful texts drop off after the first year or two following publication, even though the book continues to be used to the same extent as before. This is because of the used book market. University bookstores repeatedly buy and sell your books, cutting off publishers from sales and authors from royalties. A new edition which is justified by updated content brings a temporary respite from this unfair situation.

Other reasons to revise a textbook include your own dissatisfaction with certain sections or chapters. You may have found a better way of describing concepts or issues. You may want to improve the overall writing quality. You may want to include new and more effective illustrations. Feedback received from reviewers, instructors, and students may prompt substantive changes. Adding a coursebook, a workbook, an instructor's manual, a video- or an audiotape, an interactive computer program, a multimedia presentation, or a laboratory manual may be useful. In all such cases, a revised edition will enhance the usefulness and marketability of your text.

Successful textbooks typically are revised once every 3 to 5 years. A book may be revised sooner if advances in the discipline warrant it. Contractually, the publisher has the right to request revisions. Of course, you may suggest a revision before the publisher asks for it.

Planning Revised Editions

As you read your just published textbook, you may already think of certain improvements. Limitations often shine brighter in print than in manuscripts. If you use your text in teaching, you will have plenty of opportunities to find deficiencies and ways of improving the style, content, extent of coverage, illustrations and examples, and the like. Therefore, start thinking about ideas for revising your text as soon as possible.

Publishers send you copies of published book reviews. Study these reviews carefully. Note the positive and negative aspects of your book pointed out by the reviewers. When reviews are substantially negative, it is easy to reject them and not take the comments seriously. However, re-read the review after you have cooled off. Maybe the criticism will still seem unfair, mistaken, or due to philosophical differences that you cannot help. Nonetheless, there may be some stylistic changes that you can make that will blunt extremely negative reactions. Maybe it was how you expressed certain views, not the views themselves, that provoked strong negative reactions. If this is the case, you should revise the tone of your writing. Textbooks should help teach, and not generate controversy.

You should pay especially close attention to the reviewer who points out limitations in coverage, ambiguity in presentation, a need for more or better examples and illustrations, or lack of currency of information. These limitations are good reasons for second editions of textbooks.

Authors sometimes wonder whether to write a rebuttal to negative reviews of their books. Most journal editors allow publication of an author's rebuttal of critical reviews published in their journals. In most cases, it is better to do nothing. Nothing much can be gained by pointing out philosophical differences or differences in approaches that may have led to criticisms. However, a response may be appropriate if the reviewer makes erroneous statements about your book and you can strictly limit your response to correcting such errors.

Some textbook publishers also send out questionnaires to instructors who receive complimentary copies of your book. Some instructors fill out these questionnaires after reviewing the book, others fill them out after using the text in their teaching. The publisher then sends returned questionnaires to you. These questionnaires help assess the strengths and limitations of your text as instructors, and perhaps even students, saw them. Feedback from such questionnaires is a valuable source of information for revising and improving your text.

If the questionnaire the publisher uses needs revision or expansion to evoke more effective feedback, talk to the in-house editor. Help design an improved questionnaire that will provide you with needed information on the strengths and limitations of the text. Use this information in revising the text.

Because the main reason for revising a text is to update information, you need to keep track of research advances or significant changes in viewpoints that require timely revisions. Keep a file of recent research articles and other publications that you need to use in revising the text. Keep copies of relevant journal articles in the file. Make a list of revision ideas that occur to you and place it in the file.

You should review textbooks of other authors as they are published. You cannot forget that your product is competing with similar products on the market. Books that do not stay ahead of their competition will be eliminated from the highly competitive textbook market. Periodically, discuss the current market with your editors to plan for revised editions.

In essence, if you know how the field is changing, what competing authors are doing, and how consumers are using your book, you can produce timely revisions of your book. By making timely revisions, you also stay ahead of your competition.

Preparing Revised Editions

Discuss your ideas for the revised edition with your editors. The in-house editor needs to know if the revised book is going to be substantially different from the first edition and what kinds of new information will be included. If you plan to write one or more new chapters, the editor may have to find a technical reviewer. If the book is going to be significantly larger than the previous edition, perhaps the book will have to be priced higher. Matters such as these should be resolved before finalizing your plan for revision.

Essentially, there are two methods of preparing a revised version of a textbook. In the first method, you make changes on a printed copy of the current edition. In the second method, you revise the files on the computer disks and submit a new manuscript. The method you use depends on the amount of changes you plan to make in the existing edition.

If you plan to make only a few and minor additions or changes, update references, correct errors, and so forth, you should do it on the printed book itself. Some publishers want you to tear pages from two copies of your book; one for right-hand pages and another for left-hand pages. Occasionally, your publisher may have unbound copies of your book. If this is the case, you can obtain two unbound copies and use the right and left hand pages from them. Write corrections or additions on the printed pages themselves. If necessary, use rubber cement, paste, or tape to attach new material, but do not use paper clips. Use this method if you are making changes only in a few specific places and the number of changes is not substantial. This method will work if you simply add a summary, write new paragraphs here and there, change the year of publication of cited books to reflect recent editions, and the like. This method is desirable when a substantial amount of typeset text from the existing edition can be saved, resulting in lower cost of producing the revised edition.

If you plan to make substantial changes in the text, rewrite many sections, create new illustrations, and make stylistic changes and revise sentences throughout the book, you should prepare your revised edition on your computer. You should then submit a new manuscript of the entire book. In this case, you should follow the procedures described for submitting a new manuscript. This submission will include the original and two printed copies of your revised manuscript, computer disks containing all the chapter files, and all front and back matter.

In preparing a substantially revised edition, you still should start with your computer files of the earlier edition. In this case, you make sure that that the disks or files you use to revise contain the final, printed, version of your book. This usually is the copyedited version of your book into which you also will have entered changes made during proofreading. If you do not have the final version, ask your publisher to supply the disks that contain the final, printed version of your book.

A new chapter written for the revised edition may be handled with the first or the second method. If the new chapter is the only substantial change, you should use the first method, marking minor changes on the book pages and submitting only the new chapter on disk. You will then show minor changes on the printed pages of the earlier edition. If the new chapter is a part of more substantial changes made throughout the book, then you should use the second method. You will then submit a completely new manuscript.

■ CONCLUDING REMARKS

Textbooks are written by scholars who enjoy teaching. They know how to put ideas across well, differently, simply, elegantly, and interestingly.

They will have done this in their classrooms. A successful textbook is immensely satisfying for many reasons. The most important reason is that a text is a tool for the scholar-teacher to affect students beyond his or her classroom. Along with other scholar-teachers, the textbook writer makes a worthy contribution to the way future scientists and professionals are educated.

Preparation of manuscripts according to specified guidelines saves time, effort, and money. Authors who ignore the guidelines often are frustrated during the editorial process because of endless changes they have to make in revising the manuscript. Such authors also frustrate editors who have to repeatedly draw the author's attention to supplied guidelines. Therefore, the first step in writing a textbook is to find out what guidelines to follow. This manual contains many specific suggestions on manuscript preparation. Most of the suggestions are generic. However, you should contact your in-house or series editor to ensure that you fully understand the stylistic and other requirements of your publisher. If you follow those guidelines in preparing your first draft, you can more productively focus your attention on improving the content, coverage, and effectiveness of expression as you revise it.

Book writing and publishing are joint ventures between the author and the publisher. At the publishing house, many persons work behind the scenes to produce, publish, and market a book. Publishing houses believe in working closely with their authors. Therefore, please keep in touch with your series editor and the in-house editor.

Bibliography

■ BASIC REFERENCES ON ACADEMIC PUBLISHING

Dessauer, J. P. (1989). *Book publishing*. New York: Continuum.

Journal of Scholarly Publishing. Toronto: University of Toronto Press.

Luey, B. (1995). *Handbook for academic authors* (3rd ed.). New York: Cambridge University Press.

McDonald, S. P. (1994). *Professional academic writing in the humanities and social sciences*. Carbondale, IL: Southern Illinois University Press.

Mullins, C. J. (1977). *A guide to writing and publishing in the social and behavioral sciences*. New York: John Wiley.

Sheen, A. P. (1982). *Breathing life into medical writing: A handbook*. St. Louis, MO: C. V. Mosby.

van Leunen. M. (1978). *A handbook for scholars*. New York: Knopf.

■ BOOKS ON PREPARING ELECTRONIC MANUSCRIPTS

American Psychological Association. (1994). *Publication manual of the American Psychological Association* (4th ed.). Washington, DC: Author.

Association of American Publishers. (1983). *An author's primer to word processing*. New York: Author.

University of Chicago Press. (1987). *Chicago guide to preparing electronic manuscripts for authors and publishers*. Chicago: Author.

University of Chicago Press. (1993). *The Chicago manual of style* (14th ed.). Chicago: Author.

■ SELECTED STYLE MANUALS

American Chemical Society. (1986). *The ACS style guide: A manual for authors and editors.* Washington, DC: Author.

American Institute of Physics. (1990). *AIP style manual* (4th ed.). New York: Author.

American Mathematical Society. (1980). *A manual for authors of mathematical papers* (7th ed.). Providence, RI: Author.

American Medical Association. (1989). *American Medical Association manual of style* (8th ed.). Baltimore: Williams & Wilkins.

American Psychological Association. (1994). *Publication manual of the American Psychological Association* (4th ed.). Washington, DC: Author.

Council of Biology Editors. (1994). *Scientific style and format: The CBE manual for authors, editors, and publishers.* New York: Cambridge University Press.

Fondiller, S. H., & Nerone, B. J. (1993). *Health professionals' style book: Putting your language to work.* New York: National League for Nursing Press.

Howell, J. B. (1983). *Style manual of the English speaking world: A guide.* Phoenix, AZ: Oryx Press.

Modern Language Association. (1988). *MLA handbook for writers of research papers, theses, and dissertations.* New York: Author.

A uniform system of citation (15th ed.). (1991). Cambridge, MA: Harvard Law Review Association.

University of Chicago Press. (1993). *The Chicago manual of style* (14th ed.). Chicago: Author.

■ BOOKS ON GENERAL AND TECHNICAL WRITING

Bates, J. D. (1980). *Writing with precision.* Washington, DC: Acropolis Books.

Bernstein, T. M. (1965). *The careful writer: A modern guide to English usage.* New York: Atheneum.

Day, R. A. (1992). *Scientific English: A guide for scientists and other professionals.* Phoenix, AZ: Oryx Press.

Follett, W. (1966). *Modern American usage: A guide.* New York: Hill & Wang.

Fowler, H. W. (1987). *A dictionary of modern English usage* (2nd ed., rev.). New York: Oxford University Press.

Kirszner, L. G., & Mandell, S. R. (1986). *The Holt handbook.* New York: Holt, Rinehart & Winston.

Markland, M. T. (1983). Taking criticism — and using it. *Scholarly Publishing, 14*(2), 139–147.

Morris, W., & Morris, M. (1974). *Harper dictionary of contemporary usage.* New York: Harper.

Newman, E. (1975). *A civil tongue.* New York: Warner Books.

Strunck, W., Jr., & White, E. B. (1979). *The elements of style* (3rd ed.). New York: Macmillan.

van Leunen, M. (1978). *A handbook for scholars.* New York: Knopf.

Zinser, W. (1985). *On writing well: An informal guide to writing nonfiction* (2nd ed.). New York: Harper & Row.

■ WRITING IN NONDISCRIMINATORY LANGUAGE

American Psychological Association. (1994). *Publication manual of the American Psychological Association* (4th ed.). Washington, DC: Author.

International Association of Business Communicators. (1982). *Without bias: A guidebook for nondiscriminatory communication* (2nd ed.). New York: John Wiley.

Miller, C., & Swift, K. (1988). *The handbook of nonsexist writing for writers, editors, and speakers* (2nd ed.). New York: Harper & Row.

Moore, R. B. (1976). *Racism in the English language.* New York: Council on Interracial Books for Children/Racism and Sexism Resource Center for Educators.

■ ILLUSTRATIONS AND GRAPHICS

Council of Biology Editors. (1988). *Illustrating science: Standards for publication.* Bethesda, MD: Author.

MacGregor, A. J. (1979). *Graphics simplified: How to plan and prepare effective charts, graphs, illustrations, and other visual aids.* Toronto: University of Toronto Press.

Tufte, E. R. (1983). *The visual display of quantitative information.* Cheshire, CT: Graphics Press.

Tufte, E. R. (1990). *Envisioning information.* Cheshire, CT: Graphics Press.

■ INDEXING

Butcher, J. (1980). *Typescripts, proofs and indexes.* New York: Cambridge University Press.

Mulvany, N. C. (1994). *Indexing books.* Chicago: University of Chicago Press.

Spiker, S. (1987). *Indexing your book: A practical guide for authors.* Madison: University of Wisconsin Press.

University of Chicago Press. (1993). *The Chicago manual of style* (14th ed.). Chicago: Author.

■ PROOFREADING

American Psychological Association. (1994). *Publication manual of the American Psychological Association* (4th ed.). Washington, DC: Author.

Butcher, J. (1980). *Typescripts, proofs and indexes.* New York: Cambridge University Press.

University of Chicago Press. (1993). *The Chicago manual of style* (14th ed.). Chicago: Author.

■ SELECTED LITERARY WORKS

The following books and articles are among the few literary works with clinical and scientific significance. For the academic and professional writer, they offer good lessons in clear, simple, and attractive writing styles.

Armstrong, A. O. (1979). *Cry Babel.* Garden City, NY: Doubleday.
As the subtitle says, it is the story of "The nightmare of aphasia and a courageous woman's struggle to rebuild her life."

Bowe, F. (1981). *Comeback.* New York: Harper & Row.
An interesting book on six outstanding persons with various disabilities.

Gargan, W. (1969). *Why me?* New York: Doubleday.
The story of a person who had a laryngectomy.

Gibbs, J. M. (1973). Cleft palate babies: One mother's experience. *Nursing Care, 1,* 19–23.
A mother gives birth to a baby with cleft palate. How are the professionals handling it?

Greenberg, H. (1964). *I never promised you a rose garden.* New York: Holt, Rinehart & Winston.

Greenberg, J. (1970). *In this sign.* New York: Holt, Rinehart & Winston.
Two novels by the same author centering on persons with hearing loss.

Hodgins, E. (1964). *Episode: A report on the accident inside my skull.* New York: Atheneum.
A writer and newspaper editor describes his stroke, aphasia, and eventual recovery.

Jonas, G. (1977). *Stuttering: A disorder of many theories.* New York: Farrar, Straus, and Giroux.
A newspaper reporter known for his writing on scientific matters writes about stuttering.

Killilea, M. (1952). *Karen: A true story told by her mother.* New York: Dell.

Killilea, M. (1983). *With love from Karen.* New York: Dell.
In these two books, a mother tells a touching story of her child born with cerebral palsy. The books are an enlightening story of the family's extraordinary struggle to find help for the child.

Kopit, A. (1978). *Wings.* New York: Hill & Wang.
An outstanding play about a woman who suffers from a stroke and aphasia. A fascinating account of aphasia only a gifted literary writer could offer.

Moss, C. S. (1972). *Recovery with aphasia: The aftermath of my stroke.* Champaign, IL: The University of Illinois Press.

A professor of clinical psychology describes his stroke, aphasia, and recovery.

Park, C. C. (1982). *The siege: The first eight years of an autistic child.* Boston: Little, Brown.

A parent's view of autism; contains superb descriptions and uncommon insights.

Smithdas, R. J. (1958). *Life at my fingertips.* New York: Doubleday.

Autobiography of a writer and poet who is deaf-blind.

Smithdas, R. J. (1966). *City of the heart.* New York: Taplinger.

Poems by the same writer, poet.

Updike, J. (1987). Getting the words out. *Asha, 29,* 19-20.

A famous American author's engaging account of his stuttering.

White, E. B. (1970). *The trumpet of the swan.* New York: Harper & Row.

The story of a swan without a voice. A truly touching story of lack of communication, beautifully written for children and adults.

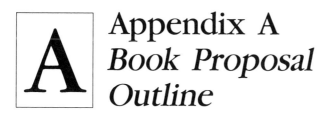

Appendix A
Book Proposal Outline

Please read Chapters 1 and 2 before writing the proposal.

AUTHORS(S)/EDITOR(S):

PROPOSED TITLE:

CONTACT AUTHOR/EDITOR:

TELEPHONE NUMBER:

WORK:

HOME:

FAX:

CORRESPONDENCE ADDRESS:

1. The philosophy of the text or the subject matter

2. The title of the book

3. The scope and audience of the book (undergraduate, graduate, dual-level)

4. Competing books on the market; their strengths and weaknesses

5. The unique features of the proposed book

6. The tentative table of contents with chapter headings and subheadings (If you have already written the book, send the manuscript with a complete table of contents.)

7. Estimated length of the manuscript

8. Number and variety of illustrations

9. Projected date of manuscript delivery

10. Vita of all authors or editors

11. Potential prepublication reviewers of the manuscript

12. Journals that may review the published book

B Appendix B
Selected Permission Forms

Authors may make copies of these forms to obtain permission from publishers, authors, models, and photographers.

REQUEST FOR PERMISSION TO REPRINT
MATERIAL FOR SCHOLARLY PURPOSES

Request sent to (publisher)

_____

_____

_____

_____

I am preparing a manuscript:

_____

(title of book)

_____

(author/editor of book)

to be published in _____ (approx. date) by

_____

(publisher's name and address)

In it I would like to include the material specified below:

Author:

Title:

Edition and date:

Figure or table number(s):

If quotation(s):

Approx. No. Words	*Pages*	*Opening Words*	*Closing Words*

I request permission to reprint the specified material in this book and in future revisions and editions thereof, for possible licensing and distribution throughout the world in all languages. If you do not control these rights in their entirety, would you please let me know where else to write. Proper acknowledgment of title, author, publisher, city, and copyright date (for journals: author, article title, journal name, volume, first page of article, and year) will be given. If the permission *of the author is also required, please supply a current address.* For your convenience, you may simply sign the release form below. A copy of this request is enclosed for your files.

Thank you.   My return address is: (please print)

Author: _____   _____

      (please print)   _____

Date: _____   _____

PERMISSION GRANTED:

_____   _____

(Signature)   (Date)

AUTHORIZATION TO REPRINT PHOTOGRAPH(S)

I, the undersigned, authorize _____ (publisher's name) to publish photograph(s) of me or _____ _____ (name of patient), identified below, as desired in professional journals and books in the interest of education, knowledge, and research.

Identification of this material in book (or journal)

_____

_____

_____

Use of material

☐ Journal article illustration   ☐ Book jacket or cover

☐ Text illustration   ☐ Advertising piece

Authorization is given to modify or retouch the aforementioned photograph(s) and to publish information relating to the case, either separately or in connection with the publication of the photograph(s).

Although I give permission for the publication for the aforementioned photograph(s) and information, it is specifically understood that I will not be identified by name.

SIGNATURE   _____
(of patient, parent, or guardian)

NAME OF PATIENT   _____

WITNESS   _____

DATE   _____

Appendix C
Author's Checklist

Check each of the following items before sending the manuscript to the editor at the publishing house:

■ TEXT

☐ The entire manuscript, including references, appendixes, tables, figures, and legends is double spaced.

☐ All headings are prepared according to the style guide specifications.

☐ Any symbols or increments of measure discussed in the manuscript that need to appear in a specific form are clearly indicated so that the copy editor can be alerted (e.g., Hz, dB, msec, etc.).

☐ All figures and tables are cited in text.

☐ Chapters of the manuscript are not stapled before sending it to the publisher. Each page is numbered.

■ FIGURES

☐ Each figure appears on a separate sheet of paper. Glossy photographs are not mounted.

☐ Figures and tables are numbered using the double digit numbering system; the first number indicates the chapter and the second number indicates the sequence of the figures within the chapter (e.g. Figure 4-1, 4-2, 4-3).

☐ Each figure has a caption that describes or explains the content of the figure, *in addition to* the explanation given in the text.

☐ Figures to be sent to the publisher are camera ready. Camera ready art includes glossy prints of a line illustration or the original line illustration prepared by the artist or printed on a high quality laser printer. *Photocopies are not camera-ready art.*

☐ Original prints of black and white photographs are enclosed. Unacceptable slides or negatives are not being sent.

☐ For line drawings taken from another publication, the actual pages from the published book or journal are enclosed.

☐ For black and white photographs taken from another publication, the original photograph is enclosed.

☐ Assessment forms and questionnaires are prepared as figures.

☐ To be camera ready, assessment forms or questionnaires are printed on a high quality laser printer.

■ TABLES

☐ All tables are double-spaced.

☐ All tables are on separate sheets of paper.

☐ All tables have titles to explain them, in addition to the explanation given in the text.

☐ All tables are numbered using the double-numbering system in which the first number indicates the chapter and the second number indicates the sequence of tables within the chapter (e.g., Table 1-1, 1-2, 1-3).

☐ Tables containing several columns have contents aligned in each column.

■ PERMISSIONS

☐ All permission forms obtained from other publishers to reprint borrowed figures, tables, or long quotations are enclosed with the manuscript.

☐ For materials taken from another source, credit lines have been typed according to the prescribed format.

☐ For a table or figure adapted from another source for which written permission is not necessary, the original source has been correctly cited to give credit (e.g., Adapted from Kelly, G. *Reading strategies.* ABC Press: Boston, 1985).

■ FRONT MATTER

☐ A final contents page has been include with the manuscript; the chapter titles in the table of contents match the chapter titles appearing in the manuscript.

☐ The person to write a foreword has been contacted (if desired) and a copy of the final manuscript has been sent.

☐ A preface has been written.

☐ Acknowledgments and/or a dedication (if desired) have been included.

☐ A contributors list (if any) has been included.

■ SENDING THE MANUSCRIPT TO THE PUBLISHER

☐ Original version plus two copies of the manuscript are being sent.

☐ Copies of the artwork are being sent.

☐ A copy of the disks containing *only* the final version of the manuscript is being sent. Disks are appropriately labeled.

☐ The manuscript is being sent by express mail or UPS Second Day delivery.

Appendix D
Reference Checklist

After you have completed your manuscript, make one last check of your reference list and the citations you have made in the text. Incomplete or incorrect citations and reference listings are common problems in textbook writing and are easier to correct the sooner they are located. Going over the checklist that follows will catch many of the most common errors or omissions made by textbook writers.

■ DO ALL CITATIONS IN THE TEXT HAVE AN ENTRY IN THE REFERENCE LIST?

If you find citations without entries in the reference list, add an entry to the reference list or delete the text citation.

■ DO ALL TEXT CITATIONS MATCH THE ENTRIES IN THE REFERENCE LIST?

Check the following:

1. Are the author names spelled the same in the citations and the reference list?
2. Is the date of publication the same in both places?
3. For publications with multiple authors, is the order of the authors' names listed the same in both places?

■ ARE CONSECUTIVE MULTIPLE CITATIONS IN TEXT ORDERED ALPHABETICALLY BY THE PRIMARY AUTHORS' NAMES?

In textbooks that include many citations, each set of citations set within parentheses should be ordered alphabetically. Have you remembered to do this throughout the text?

■ ARE THERE ENTRIES IN THE REFERENCE LIST THAT HAVE NOT BEEN CITED IN THE TEXT?

If there are, add a text citation for the reference or delete the reference entry.

■ ARE THE ENTRIES IN THE REFERENCE LIST ORDERED ALPHABETICALLY BY THE PRIMARY AUTHOR'S LAST NAME?

Recheck your alphabetizing. Also make sure that multiple entries for the same author are ordered by date, from earliest to latest publication.

■ ARE ALL ENTRIES IN THE REFERENCE LIST COMPLETE?

Go over each reference entry carefully for obvious omissions or errors. They will be much easier to spot at this stage than several weeks or months later in the publication process.

Some of the most commonly omitted items include:

1. The page numbers of chapters contributed to edited books.
2. The month of publication (in addition to the date) in references to unpublished presentations made at conferences and symposia. (The city where the conference or symposium was held also is frequently omitted.)
3. Update entries listed as "in press" as soon as they are published.

Appendix E
Most Commonly Used Proofreader's Symbols

ℒ or ℽ   delete; take it out

⌒   close up; print as o̮ne word

or ⟩   insert a̬space

ᴄℊ #   space ᴗevenly ᴗwhere ᴗshown

+r   tras̬npose; reverse orde⁀t the⁀

/   used to separate two or more marks and often used as a conclud-
ing stroke at the end of an insertion

⌐   ⌐ set farther to the left

＝   fix align͞m͟e͟n͟t͞

‖   ‖ straighten or align

✗   imperfect or broken character

▢   indent or insert em space

𝖰   begin a new paragraph

(ˢᵖ)   spell out (set 5 (lbs) as five pounds)

cap   set in capitals (CAPITALS)

sm cap   Set in small capitals (SMALL CAPITALS)

ital   set in italic (*italic*)

rom   set in roman (roman)

bf   set in boldface (**boldface**)

lc   set in lowercase (lowercase)

lc   set in LOWERCASE (lowercase)

$=$ or /H/   hyphen

1/N or /N/   en dash (1965-1972)

1/M or /M/   em — or long — dash

V   superscript or superior (as in a $\times$ b²)

Λ   subscript or inferior (₂ as in H_2O)

     comma

     apostrophe

     period

     parentheses

[ ]   brackets

wf   wrong font; a character or word in the wrong size or style

: or ⊙   colon

" " or ' '   quotation marks

Index